I0150166

Pages of a Broken Diary

by Toti O'Brien

Copyright © 2022 by Toti O'Brien

Cover Design: Pski's Porch
Layout: Pski's Porch

All rights reserved. No part of this book may be reproduced in any form by any electronic or mechanical means including photocopying, recording, or information storage and retrieval without permission in writing from the author.

ISBN-13: 978-1-948920-28-5
ISBN-10: 1-948920-28-X

for more books, visit Pski's Porch:
www.pskisporch.com

Printed in U.S.A.

you can be a stranger anywhere...

Contents

Pages
of a Broken Diary

AWAKE

The sharp tip of a feather pricks my chin, piercing through the fabric. My comforter must have thinned out. Still, it comforts me. Half asleep, I pull it over my face, brushing my cheek against its softness. But the tip of a feather awakes me with its light sting. Hazy, under eyelids closed, I see a running goose. It must be the one whose down fills this blanket, my sweet bed companion.

I see it briskly beheaded, on a sunny day, body frantically touring the patio while the neck spills blood like a broken faucet. Almost a circus number, leaving children eerily stupefied.

How can a bird run without cerebral matter? Well, there wasn't much to start with. But how can a corpse keep going? Shouldn't it fall like a stringless puppet?

Smoky concepts. Let's see, residual momentum? Say the nervous impulse has to complete its path, bring its message to the far extremities, although the source is gone. The extremities, alas, do not know.

Scary, is it, such delay of information? Where is the bird going? What is it running from and where to? Why this silly dance? Disaster has already stricken, old clown. Don't you see you are dead?

The goose sees, but it takes a while. That's all.

I would like to sleep a bit more. I'm not ready to plunge into daylight. To invite back relaxation, to ignite reverie I picture your hand on my breast, using mine as a momentary ersatz. That is how I realize my breast has changed over time. Like the blanket, it has thinned. I'm afraid it would not fill your palm as it used to, and such passing thought saddens me.

Though… there are ways to gather the flesh, hold it up, make it bloom into a small but satisfactory mound, nipples pulled out and squeezed between my, your fingertips.

Wait. Right there, my flesh hosts extraneous formations I had forgotten about. Briskly, they come to mind. They get frequently checked to verify if they evolved into lethal stuff, ready to be butchered away, or not yet. The outcome, as well as the timing, is unpredictable.

My breasts, like myself, are bound on uncertain course to unknown destination. Maybe they are dancing a last dance this morning, are they? I'm not all that different from a crazed headless goose—my deceased bedmate, slowly wasting away, still keeping me warm.

GENESIS

Women came mostly in pairs.

Maybe not always. Still, I remember several sets of two. Sisters, and one is more beautiful than the other, I register with a slight discomfort. There's unbalance, there's lack of symmetry in the ways of destiny or life.

Well, I know little of destiny. The whole concept is too imbued of past and future for me to understand. I am barely managing a timid present. I don't know lots about life, but you need a kind of container, an overall frame, a recipient wherein you can throw miscellanea just as I toss my toys into a wicker crate, at night, promising that I'll sort them tomorrow.

I have noticed this sister-thing tends to repeat itself. It occurs in a loop. I know two sisters, for instance, the prettiest of whom didn't marry, while the other did and had two daughters, the prettiest of whom won't marry, while the other will (this prodigy is still in the making, but I'll see it unfold as I grow up, as I keep observing).

How is this possible? I have already ascertained prettiness gets you love. The concept has been hammered especially in fairy tales, yet it doesn't hold water. Something must be at play, so powerful it overturns beauty's rule. What? I am clueless. Should I ask? I have, once or twice. Why didn't X (or X_1, her niece) marry? Replies are so evasive they confirm my suspicions. Something mighty and mysterious is at work, puzzling, vaguely alarming.

Pretty loners and plain spouses have still much in common, though the spinsters harbor a martyred and melancholy smile while the wedded ones have ruddy matter-of-fact expressions. They all wear black and their chests are sunken.

Which has nothing to do with their breast size, not supposed to be appraised anyway, unless so imposing it can't be possibly ignored. Wide or small-breasted, women here have caved-in chests, as if breathing were painful—had been since early childhood, perhaps since day one.

Chests are compressed, squeezed, all buttoned-up—an invisible weight bending the top vertebrae, as if burden had been dealt by whoever organized the game in an ever so slight disproportion. The female population having been overloaded, just going from sunrise to sundown unavoidably shrinks a girl's vital sap, crushing her ribcage, lowering her sternum, fostering a beaten pose of resignation.

Will this happen to me? I have reasons to suspect it will, that I marry or not. There's no difference. But my lack of familiarity, I said, with destiny prevents me from a clear sense of cause and effect, therefore I don't panic. Not quite. I avoid prophecies, worries, anticipation.

Eager for distraction, weary of the dimly lit interiors where females are confined (is lack of oxygen, after all, what collapses their lungs?) I run outside, in the orchards and fields, over wooded hills, across sand beaches.

There is where men are, besides at the bar, but that only applies to the evening hour and to festive occasions.

Men don't wear black except for church or funerals. They wear working hues, dark and dull, browns or greys. In the fields, on the boats, in the orchards, in the pastures they are mostly alone. Sometimes they sing to themselves. Otherwise they are silent.

I am well aware those males found in nature are to be avoided because virtually dangerous to females, especially under age. I know they can do you things, and before I learn of which kind I have intuited they belong to the aggressive, harmful, painful domain.

Yet I can't avoid meeting men as I explore my surroundings. Like trees, boats, clouds, fruit, bird or fish they are a prominent feature of the giant container—life, for lack of a better term.

Men are busy. So are women unless they make coffee, pour it in ridiculously small china cups then sip it so slowly, you understand its very function is to still time, keep them idle for a minute. To the same purpose men light and smoke cigarettes, briefly putting down whatever tool they were symbiotically embracing. They take a sit, suck, inhale, puff out, stare at nothing.

Men I meet in my lone discovery tours are fishermen, shepherds, hunters, lumberjacks, mostly peasants. All of them, but peasants especially, are intent at something steadily forcing them to look down. Their skin is thick and tanned, leathery. Their eyes, when they lift them because a naïf, stupid town-girl dares to say hi, are invariably blue. This doesn't happen to women, go see why.

Watery, yet not reminiscent of the ocean, which is denser, full of purple and green, theirs is the pale ceruleum of the sky. All the peasants I know have azure irises, innocent, lost, riveted to the rich brown of dry lava they labor nonstop as life demands of them, because that's what life does.

ISLAND

I understood. Finally.

First, the smell of the sea. Then the smell of fish, so intense that along with the smell of bread it meant life itself. Then the fragments of rope, the consistency of the sail, so sheer in the light, so solid to the touch.

I understood the sense of abandonment and where it came from. The terror of losing the one I loved most, each time that he left. The uncertainty of his return. And the worship of the boat shielding him from the elements, bringing him home unscathed, once again.

Now I knew why the harbor, the lighthouse, the foghorn had such appeal. I had been the fisherman's wife before, as were my mother, my mother's mother. Yes, yes, all the way back. Deep into the memory of the island, buried by the sand and pebbles I trod on as a child, while I stared into a blueness only whispering freedom and possibilities, silent about its secret essence.

I had not learned, yet, how to spell the word loss.

But it was engraved in my cells, soaked my arteries and veins. It just needed to unspool like a fishing line from its reel, my heart hooked at its tip. My heart already harpooned, quietly bleeding.

THE TREE

When did it pop out? How did I miss it so far? Once a week, I cross this bridge back and forth. I am sure my eyes met it a trillion times, without carrying the impression to the main switchboard (my brain or at least its conscious department).

Here it is, now. Small tree stuck among the bars of the parapet, a few twigs stretched towards the asphalt—fingers trying to grasp something—the soft crown perched into the void, suspended over the chasm, overlooking fourteen freeway lanes.

It's no more than a fluffy ball, deep green, enlivened by a sprinkle of pale younger leaves. But there's something gripping about it. I can't just pass by, walk away. Feelings are stirred more than I would expect. This tree makes me cringe.

Its squeezed attitude almost reeks of discomfort. I know branches don't hurt... In fact, I don't know. They sure twist and twirl better than limbs do. Still, while forcing their way through those posts they exude a manner of stress. A spasm, almost.

The imbalance is disturbing as well. The precariousness. The impudent diagonal, heading for a fall, I am sure. Though it won't happen, of course. Trees are well attached to the ground.

Where is hard to see. Clearly, this one has roots into the pavement of the bridge, which looks kind of exiguous but not paper-thin. There are bricks and mortar and stuff where vegetation can dwell, more or less. This tree did, then found its way upward, looking for a manageable future in the middle of nowhere.

It is not in the middle. I have verified. Technically, the tree stands two thirds in. Or out... bridges are confusingly reversible. Not only it is asymmetrical on a perpendicular plane (the big eccentric tuft disproportioned to the scant inward growth), but sagittally as well.

Still, because of an optical illusion it manages to look central. As I said, in the middle of nowhere. Does it perceive the inappropriateness of its posture? The intrinsic hopelessness of its location? Plants don't feel. Well, they feel some things, light for instance, since they grow in its direction. Water, which roots dig no matter how deep. Maybe that is all, light and water.

In such case why worry? The tree hasn't a clue about its sad isolation and dramatic exposure. It doesn't register the absence of its kin or of its neighbor creatures, the animals. I haven't seen bird or butterfly ever rest on its branches, but it's me who link those disparate entities in coherent tableaux. I am the one missing something. They don't.

I believe the tree doesn't smell the exhausts rising from the hell of engines and tar, underneath. Smog will slowly tarnish its leaves, but they will not notice.

Still, I can't just walk by. Trouble gets hold of me. Is it a resonance? This absurd shard of life stuck among rails suggests a lone human being, maybe assailed by a tempting desire, ready for a last decision yet torn, pulled in opposite ways. To be or not. To jump…

The tree is not a person. Plants are not suicidal. Never heard of anything of the kind. Actually, what makes it impossible not to be compelled by the tree's sight is the very opposite. The most powerful call, the deepest emotional echo is aroused by the absurdity of its impulse to live. By the nerve of such impromptu thriving in the uncanniest of places.

A place technically inexistent, a transit overlooking a transit. If this brave exploit of vitality should communicate enthusiasm, it's heartbreaking instead. It is tearing. Acute. Bittersweet. Forlorn.

How did this happen? As always, with a seed and a crack in the wall. A sexual intercourse at its most banal. Spontaneous. Mindless. Barbarous.

A flying seed finds a crack and it can't resist. No matter where it belongs a crack is a crack, period. A seed knows how it feels to be inside it, cozy, snug and just in the right place. That is all a seed wants and it is enough.

Only a regular intercourse, uncaring of sequels as most are. Probably prompted by the wind, that slut of all sluts. The wind (master of mischief, thief, voyeur) carried the seed into the crack, then resumed its flight. It didn't come back to witness the birth of the incongruous, the lone bridger perched over the ravine but not even fit to write its own tags, its own poetry, its own revolt.

The wind doesn't come back. This, now shaking the trunk as if to uproot it for good, is another wind that remembers nothing. This gush, making leaves shiver as if a fever were burning them, is not yesterday's.

No one visits, truly, but trees don't know of solitude. They don't mind estrangement. They take what they get.

BRONTE

When I hear the word Bronte, two British girls come to mind. Women writers, and of course windy hills, heather, northern romance.

Bronte is not an English name, though. Born South, under a volcano, it means "rumble." It refers to the moaning guts of our mother earth when she's discontent, about to erupt lava on her kids.

Bronte is a verdant feud the Spanish gave to the British, disregarding the fact that the inhabitants weren't Spanish or British. The land was handed down like a precious stone, green with olives and grapes, starred with the gold of citrus trees.

It's a shame that due to fake promises of justice, alas, only meant to ease the negotiation, riots flared beyond control and some well-off people were killed. Do I feel for them? Yes. The slaughtering of civilians is called a massacre.

I ask myself if their living a quite leisurely life prior to their untimely death is a mitigating factor. I guess not. Is it normal to be born into privilege and deem it right? Stick to it, keep it tight, display it with arrogance in the face of dire need? It must be, as I don't see many exceptions to the rule. Therefore the rich folks in question were no criminals. They should not have been slayed.

What about the five peasants shot against a wall, the day after? None of them to later inquiry was proved guilty of anything. All bore the same first name, matched with an assortment of local patronymics. Was it by chance?

They were all named Nunzio, which signifies "angel." Is there meaning behind the coincidence? Does history still itself, for a second, if we dare repeating these names out loud, calmly spelling these five letters five times?

What about the fifth Nunzio, whom none of the soldiers dared to shoot? He was the village fool, and a boy. Even feuds the Spanish donated to the

English have fools, neither Spanish nor English, of course.

No one fired at the fool, but he didn't realize it. Not quite.

When he found himself still alive—was he, truly?—he kneeled down and wept, arms thrust towards the sky. He cried tears of joy, muttering thanks to the Virgin who, knowing him innocent, had graced him. Knowing him sinless, pure, incapable of evil, Mary-Mother-of-God had protected him. She had kept him unscathed.

On his knees, he sang praises, under the scorching sun of the dusty plaza that Goya would have painted, for sure, if he were around, when the General-of-Our-Resurgence arrived and took care of things. He hovered above the kid like an eagle, then cold-bloodedly shot him in the head.

Is it what makes a hero? I wonder, as I have honored the man as such since elementary school. His name was printed in bold, etched in stone, a pride of the nation. Is it what true heroism means?

What about the lawyer who wasn't called Angel but, being Bronte's most educated fellow, should be kept under cautious control. Accused of riotous intentions, he was jailed. He still waited for his verdict when news came of his complete uninvolvement, and he was released on parole. His friends begged him to leave. He remained for justice to take its course. He was shot for good measure.

I never saw his name on a street plaque, not even an alley.

MY FATHER'S SCREAM

The only time I got worried," she says, "is when during the wake I heard your father yell. That long animal howl really scared me."

She is the family friend who is also a physician, sure to stick around during the funeral, Diazepam in her purse, alert, ready to deliver instructions, call an ambulance.

The old folks need watching, of course. An uncle has fainted as soon as he has arrived to church. A few steps up the nave, never reached his pew. Take his pulse, fetch a glass of water, shove him into a taxi, go, go!

Luckily, no further incidents have plagued the ceremony so far.

"I was truly alarmed," she insists, "when he suddenly bent—hands grasping the rail, knees buckling below him—and let out that wild wail, unstoppable."

"You should take traditions into account," I add to mitigate her reaction, dull her shock. "Screaming before the dead is part of our southern lifestyle."

I remember Dad's mom at her husband's burial. She, always modest, shy, buttoned up, made quite a display. Yelling like a slaughtered swine, she attempted to throw herself inside the open hole where the coffin had been lowered, not yet covered with dirt. Of course she was held back, but she managed to engage in a furious struggle with those trying to contain her, in a sudden explosion of rage and despair.

But I don't describe such gruesome scene to the family doctor. No need.

She dismisses, anyway, my hypothesis of cultural influences over Father's manifestation of grief. Local habits, she affirms, can't explain it. Not so far away. Not in such a different context. Does she mean "in absence of witnesses able to correctly appreciate"?

Perhaps she is right. I don't know, because I wasn't present. Didn't hear Father's scream.

I can hear it now, very distinctly, in my imagination.

I can tell (could tell even the doctor) how it felt, because it echoes mine. The abrupt, ugly sound I uttered when the mournful news reached me on the phone.

I recall the cell on my bed, where it slipped from my hand as I slipped somewhere lower, not sure where. On the floor, I guess. I remember banging at the mattress—open palms? closed fists?—my arms groping in search of support or resistance, as my dad's reached for the wooden rail.

I remember an unarticulated lament, awful. A long, indistinct vowel.

"He yelled like an animal," our doctor friend comments. She loves beasts. Her tone is compassionate, sympathetic. Like an animal, though the incomprehensible verse has a rather exact significance. It means "no." The most useless of words. The most helpless.

It means "no" when we know that such syllable won't change a thing, yet everything should be changed. It means the kind of "no" claiming to subvert the progress of time, to upset natural laws.

I'm not sure if such utterance of sheer revolt can be defined animal. Surely it isn't godly. I suspect it to be quintessentially human.

IMPRESSIONS

Like a stain, adrenaline tints my thighs. Inner side. Stretching over… seven inches perhaps? I never measured it. Spreading left and right in roughly shaped butterfly wings, clumsy half moons, like a Rorschach card.

I don't see it, of course. I sense it to the tiniest detail. Every pixel is burning with pain.

Although it is very acute, the throb isn't red. It is yellow. A dark shade, as for some kind of beer. Golden. Amber. Neither warm nor attractive. Rather acrid. Like urine.

Like urine, adrenaline is unavoidable.

Truly, I have no idea of what it is. Someone mentioned adrenaline when I was in school. Someone—teacher? smart mate? can't recall—said: "Adrenaline fills your blood and drenches your muscles when you are caught in a rush of anger or fear." When you want to fight or to flee but can't choose which one.

So, I have given a name to this fever always biting the same corner of me, drawing a yellow map, the color of danger. Dots and dots, lines, peaks, creases. Like a cardiac or an encephalic tracing. Only, in the wrong place. Only, carved into my flesh rather than printed on paper. A Morse message (on the chatty side) spat out of an obsolete telegraph machine.

The area isn't close to my crotch. Sexual feelings are absent. And it isn't close to my knees. Sort of half way. It does not reach my thighs' outer edges. It remains circumscribed. Not less excruciating.

It engorges my thighs when I'm angry or fearful. When I was angry. I am not anymore. Why was I? I'm sure the reasons were tenuous. Things might have occurred that I had found unfair, causing visceral, abrupt feelings of revolt I couldn't express. Such vibes gathered in my lower body: "Here we are, in case you needed to know." I could have been spared the information, since acting upon it was barred. I guess, slowly the lesson sank in. "Let go," I whispered to whatever soaked me, "It matters little. Rage is utterly unfashionable. Drop it."

Now the thing only strikes under pretext of terror. Phone ringing in the middle of night. Sound of steps in the lone house. I have misplaced my purse, my wallet was stolen. Seldom chance, rare occasions, of course.

Or in dreams. Bad ones happen. Haunted cities. Underworlds. War zones. Killers, robbers. A loved one disappearing, in danger. Endless, bitter, vain family quarrels. Pain awakes me, fiercely stabbing my skin though it sits deeper—a bone marrow disease.

Crucified on the mattress, unable to move, I wait for the yellow light to wash off my body. It takes time. When it's gone, echoes linger. Tissues remain sore as if scarred. Muscles ache as if from too much exertion. I wish it were true. I wish I had run, swum across a river, escalated a mountain. I have done nothing. Adrenaline did it. Ancient rituals. Souvenirs of the wild.

Please. No enemy is here, no threat is in view. These are nightmares. I shouldn't have to fight ghosts. "Don't get all worked up," I say to my neurons, synapses, hormones, the entire apparatus. "We live in a civilized world. Rage and stress have been managed. Phobia analyzed. Past trauma resolved," I explain to my cells.

But they have a mind of their own.

UNCAGED

It's a summer night and the mice are restless. Their noise drives me crazy.

The cage is in the kitchen but all doors are open. We need air. Mice are active at night, like hamsters or guinea pigs. I'm used to some rumpus… it almost conceals my sleep. But tonight they are outrageous.

I can't help bursting: "What's wrong with the beasts?" My child's voice echoes from his room (our house is pocket-sized): "They are making love, Mom." I hold my breath for a minute and then I start laughing, struck by a surreal vision: "Do you mean these are bedsprings squeaking?" That's exactly the noise, though it must be produced otherwise. Suddenly I remember field trips, cheap hotels, flimsy drywalls and everlasting love symphonies. I don't think my son pictures anything of the kind, but he firmly insists: "They are having sex, Mom."

Though I missed any warning sign, a week later babies are born. I am stunned both by the rise of my kitchen's population (five miniature toys sucking from reclined, contented, triumphing Mama) and my child's premonition.

Nothing I can do, but watch. I feed the couple as usual. Mommy will take care of the kids. Nothing to do but watch, and that's how I notice. I almost step on it, and it's me now squeaking and squealing. One of the newly born is out of the cage.

Passing through the bars, of course, is no feat. The thing isn't thicker than my finger. It progresses across the kitchen floor, heading opposite to where the cage is. Heading nowhere, in fact… I doubt it has the faintest sense of directions. It must be blind still. But it advances, oh wonder, in a perfect straight line, without hesitation.

They came in a rainbow of shades, dark brown to snow white. Maybe this one is hazel, or gray, some in-between nuance. Its appearance doesn't impress me. Its speed does, I mean its incredible slowness. The mouse moves like a slug. In fact, even slower. But its pace is regular, constant, as if an alien force, an invisible hand were steadily pushing it.

My mind isn't fast either at grasping the meaning of this. Is the mouse lost? It isn't. Blind or not, its sense of smell is quite strong. It knows where Mom and the rest of the gang are.

It is getting away. This baby is sick, weak, malformed. It won't steal milk from its healthy bros. It is not meant to live, and it knows. I'm aware of such hardwired behaviors. I was told that Mom gives the signals... She refuses to feed the unfit one, she shrugs, shoves it off.

I cannot confirm. All I see is baby on the go, dragging its tiny paws as if lifting stones for a pyramid, sliding forwards one inch per hour or less. Three times, as in spite of common sense I keep bringing it back, placing it kind of casually in the bunch. Don't ask why. I know it's a lost cause and not my freaking business. I know it's hopeless.

When I see it engaged once more in its personal Odyssey, I understand I should let destiny take its course.

I can't fathom why baby keeps moving, with an effort that must be Herculean as it hasn't sucked a single drop since its birth. Why doesn't it lie in a corner? Where is it bound?

The only possible "where" is "away." Why is away so mighty and so far?

Does it have to move out of Mom's sight? Perhaps. Many animals hide when they sense death coming. Instinct tells them.

Instinct talks to baby mouse, just born but not quite. Just born, yet a million-year-old, heavy-loaded with pain, rejection, exile. Instinct whispers the old litany in those quasi-invisible ears. Meekly, baby grabs and shoulders its cross, here, on my kitchen floor.

I am not ready. I'm not sure I can witness this. Let me step into another room, think of something else.

I don't know when and where it dissolves. I can't find the corpse. I have left the door to the patio wide open. The grass is very tall in my kerchief of a garden. Summer hasn't withered it yet. It smells pungent, alive. To a mouse it smells like a forest. Baby mice have a strong olfactory system, even those who will not survive. Their sense of smell guides them.

I have left the garden door open, mouse.

GARDENS

A remote corner of the land was named "the three gardens." "Upper," "under," and "under-under," they led into each other like Russian dolls. No independent access was there for second an third. Like matryoshkas, they also got smaller.

Part of the labyrinthine structure of the property (sparse with groves, creeks, small bridges of imprecise nature) they were once designed with care. They comprised flowerbeds, as few elaborate bricks testified, peering through the lace of wild vegetation.

They smelled good. In the lowest, a mimosa tree stood proud and tall, striving for visibility as climbers, unleashed, tried to gobble it up. Tiny yellow balls flew everywhere, honey-sweet and yet kind of suffocating (I distrusted yellow, a slightly dangerous hue).

In the upper garden, small violets hid by the mighty trunks of palm trees, their perfume veiled and velvety. I was thrilled by the way leaves submerged the blooms, making them invisible until I finally caught them. I was taught how to squeeze them into letters, send them to missing Mom. The intensity of the scent calmed my longing.

The three gardens were connected by steps. Large stones, barely juxtaposed, shook a bit more with each passing season. I climbed carefully, all senses alert, to avoid tripping and dragging rocks into my fall.

I must have spent eternity upon those stairs, judging by how sharply I recall them. They ran through the entire property and the more I grew the more I explored, trusting both my sense of orientation and my taste for disorientation.

The land was a living soul of multiple personalities. It contained a chorus of voices (my fantasies, tales I read, new stories I invented) endlessly entertaining me in conversation, like my feet and legs knowing no boredom, no exhaustion. I spent all day wandering with a sandwich, a hat and a stick.

Not yet. Back to the gardens. Such a perfect haven, Grandma thought, for my toddler promenades. Searching memory (so lazy in details) a parasol appears out of nowhere and I feel the pressure of heat, the weight of sunbeams (again, yellow). A vertigo, as if number three, deepening, sinking into the earth, figured infinity. I recall the excitement of secret. Weren't those plots terra incognita? Difficult to reach, impossible to be seen if not one by one, hidden behind each other like violets under their leaves.

Mystery was enhanced, if possible, by the state of abandonment of the place, its incongruous inutility. Why was nobody there? The question, without need for formulation, pulled out of their virtual box a bunch of mechanic figurines rushing down scrambled paths, peering behind the greenery, waving coquettish hands before vanishing. Why was such paradise eaten by wilderness?

No melancholy accompanied those remarks. I'm not sure I knew yet what sadness was. I was puzzled by the layering of tenses, past and present so weirdly intertwined. By the consciousness of something revolved, the persistency of its trace.

Later, the graveyard, just a wall apart, would provide the one word I missed. Later, the graveyard, next door, would hand me the key.

NICOTINE

When I work with my favorite clay (Jamaica, with its chocolate hue, its rich, dense, oily consistency) my hands get a brown stain soap doesn't dissolve. Nothing permanent. It gradually vanishes by itself. But I find my temporary tan kind of pleasant.

It reminds me of my two grandfathers. Both chain smokers, one died of lung cancer at age sixty-nine and the other much later, of tobacco-unrelated causes. Cigarettes, held by index and thumb, squeezed against the middle finger, were responsible for the ocher taint of their skin, here more yellow, there darker.

My grandpas didn't share a same background. One was lower class, metalsmith by trade. The other was an engineer. He got down and dirty anyway, on construction sites, in the orchards. He cut wood and pruned, churned and shoveled concrete.

I loved those large, patched, multicolored hands I trustfully held. They looked gorgeous. They meant capability, experience. They were active, savvy. Continuous work peeled and scratched them, digging fields and creases where nicotine dwelled. Labor and cigarettes seemed indivisible, a whole, worthy of awe and loaded with authority.

Smoke only engraved men's fingers.

Although workingwomen had rough hands—I knew well their touch, their grip and their briskness—their skin was thick, red, but not stained. They rarely smoke and I wonder why. Butts were found in workshops, in stables and fields but not in the kitchen, the sewing, the laundry room. Was there any practical reason? I doubt it.

Rich women did smoke. Like locomotives, to be exact. I noticed it on accompanying Grandma to see wealthy relatives who held weekly salons. Fair ladies, with hair dyed and curled, briefly smiled down at me. In a blurred-yet-creepy nightmare I recall beringed, high-heeled figures sparkling with nail polish and gold. They greeted me with gaiety loaded with something damp, something teary, always a plaintive note in their voice.

Grand-aunts, second cousins, I never figured out what they were. They stood up at my arrival like jacks-in-the-box, then regained their place on the sofa and forgot about me. I recall giant couches in luxury flats crowded with carpets, thick curtains, huge light fixtures and enormous floral displays, things strange and superfluous.

Those reunions involved card games, munching, drinking, lots of gossip punctuated by relentless smoking. But those hands, occasionally reaching me for a caress, weren't stained. Was their skin too compact and smooth? Tightly woven, like silk, perfectly sealed. Nicotine couldn't break the surface.

Lipstick, on the contrary, rimmed the niveous wrap of thin cigarettes flooding marble ashtrays. I lingered on those pretty shades, coral, purple, vermillion and pink, sucking them with my eyes as if they were candy.

Bored upper-class ladies smoke while they spoke evil of their husbands, who of course weren't present. They were not excluded, just busy otherwise. The oldest and dullest men attended for lack of alternatives, tiny, faded silhouettes shielded by humongous newspapers.

Spouse-related complaint was so steady an activity, practiced with such gusto, I, while offering to the conversation a distracted ear, subconsciously assumed husbands were a kind of plague, striking randomly and for undetermined reasons. Widespread, and quite hard to shake off.

All of them apparently acted in similarly obnoxious manners (the detail of which I omitted to realize, part because I didn't care, part because of abrupt volume drops). Luckily, those choral laments seemed to bring relief by mutual support, by kin solidarity before a common disgrace. Shared pain became lesser pain. While they echoed each other, the wives grew merrier. More intent to the game of bridge, delighted by fine pastries, by the anisette they sipped in miniature glasses.

They kept smoking.

My dad, the son of a metalsmith, studied.

He did not smoke. He didn't work either. Sure, he read and wrote, which were income-making activities, but it took me a while to realize it. Dad's hands were white, small, plump and conical, neither roughened nor stained. I had my personal reasons for treating them cautiously.

Mom and both grandmothers never touched a cigarette. They were often sad. Melancholic, the three of them. I wonder if such mood was due to a lack of tobacco.

In our Southern, archaic, retrograde little town, a female smoking by herself in the street was a whore. Lighting a cigarette while you waited, let's say, for a date in front of a bar wasn't the best idea. An old code, universally accepted yet unspoken. No one told me. It did not take me long to figure it out.

My grandfathers lit their next cigarette with the previous one. They were busy men, busy smoking. Large hands, scarred. Milky nails like abalone shells. Their palms a geography of marks—mountains, craters, dirt roads, riverbeds. Hands like moons. Like fertile mud.

When my hands resemble those for a while, I breathe deeper. They have become rare, endangered. Soon extinct.

WRITER

When you sat there at four in the morning, having quietly slipped out of your bedroom.

When you sat there and wrote, thoughts like threads of cobwebs, like a minute procession of ants. Like black hieroglyphs, sharp like blades. Like miniaturized barbed wire, iron against snow.

When you sat and your head was a cube, your head was a pyramid, your head was a building, your face a façade. And your face was leather, was parchment, your face was a library. Your eyes, turned inwards, fell back into your skull, that obscure recess, that cavernous catacomb full of cavities, teaming with archeological remains, broken amphorae, broken steles.

From that cave of silence and resonance, your eyes sent a beam piercing the predawn dusk to reach a distant landscape. Maybe a castle small like a matchbox, or a mountain, maybe a church the size of a saltshaker, or a steeple, its bell faintly chiming. What did your eyes see? Perhaps nothing, while your thumb and index were wagging your lead like a helm, ink bravely navigating the page, a soft petrol tide.

Father, when you sat there, antelucan, heavy-lidded, night owl blinking at daylight, you hadn't eaten a thing since your modest dinner of the evening before. You consigned to the chair, desk, paper and pen your newly born emptiness, consciousness un-bitten, dry tongue, pink-sore gums, teeth small like those of a kitten.

You pulled out of your head—of the vacuity at the root of your nose, hyphenating your brow—a clean rope stripped of fleshy tenderness. Lines sharpened by the lucidity of hunger, tensed with the despair of weakness. Lines like arrows piercing your stomach, your guts.

Afterwards, you showered and went to Mass. On your way back you bought the newspaper. Then you drank a small cup of coffee, having stirred in it a teaspoon of sugar. Sip by sip, left hand gripping the edge of the kitchen table. Slowly breaking the fast.

IN TONGUES

When they asked me which one of the Norse brothers…

I cannot be specific, especially since they switched places. Otherwise, they were uncannily kind—because I couldn't make out their cursing, of course. They were swearing, I'm sure, as all packs of brothers do while driving a rented vehicle in traffic across cities unknown.

But I didn't pay heed to their interactions, busy enough with the one who was momentarily closest to me. Beltless, I lost my balance at each funambulic turn the van managed. My cheek ended against the large palm of the nearest brother, always ready, and courteous at that, to secure my uprightness. What a strange sort of thrill, my face in his hand. No hand of mine was involved, as I deem it a body part to be sparely used. Only one at a time, please, no matter whose, or else all becomes granted, all gets spoiled in a blink.

Was it dusk? Hard to say. Light is gloomy in the back of a crowded van. I was holding the guidebook and vainly trying to decipher it. It kept crumbling away. For how long had Mom stored it? Why was everything we owned obsolete? Worse… why did it all fall apart? On its own, no one being at fault, just because of some ineluctable doom? That, I couldn't bear.

Pages disintegrated through my fingers like petals of long-dead blooms—pointedly, violets—before I could read the addresses of the Museums we looked for. After all, this was a cultural journey. The Norse brothers weren't here for vacations. They needed, urged to know. But I couldn't get a single street name, and felt terrible. They kept laughing, unscathed.

A flash lit my brain, then. The Museum of Justice. I thought I could get us there. Would it… would they be interested? Such a modern concept. Although I realized it exhibited, mostly, tokens of injustice. Oh, well. Proofs of human cruelty and manmade suffering. Public horrors. Then, how could we reach it on time if it was dusk, already? Evening, when it starts falling, tends to quickly precipitate.

And I wondered, while the dark gulped us down, if what I couldn't forgive Mom for was just that—being a Viking, being fair and blond while I (the poor bastard) belonged to the other side of the family, she affirmed. But you can't belong to one side, Mother dear. Look at your hand. You can't split the palm from the back without making a bloody mess, still ending with another sort-of-palm, sort-of-back. You cannot divide sides, only multiply them, and that doesn't help.

So which one of the Norse brothers, that night, was called Thor, or Thorwald, or Thorwaldson? I'd say none of them, but I didn't ask. Did I care? No one in my family was ever called Thor, except for a distant cousin. That's why I kept my hands to myself in the van, no matter how dizzy I got.

2. When they asked me which one of the Dane's movies I preferred, of course I preferred them all. But then, *Melancholia*.

That one I found so uplifting, I kept playing it back in my brain for several centuries. It figured out the death-issue, which I had thought unsolvable. Because what makes death scary if not lack of simultaneousness? Two things only are unpleasant about it. One is loss, on account of the bereaved. Fundamentally selfish, yet scorching all the same. Loss is a bunch of neurons previously attached to the passed one, now hanging loose like electrical wires uncovered, uncapped, and each time we brush them we get a hell of a shock. The other pain is less intimate, more mature, yet still raw. It's the sadness of what the deceased has missed and we enjoy, call it possibilities, life in general. The great show that unblinkingly goes on while someone has been unjustly kicked out. What if the whole show ends, with due applauses and bows? Then nobody gets fired. No room for regrets. What is death without survivors? Nothing at all.

Then I think of those extinct societies whose last members starved to death or indulged in cannibalism—which instead of a ferocious deed might have been a merciful act, between euthanasia and communion. Because what is best? To die a bit later, bit earlier? Does it count, when there is no future? Does it matter, when aching so bad?

When they starved or they froze or succumbed to plagues, frankly, who wanted to be last? Had I come by and asked who among them was called Thor, or Thorwald, as I looked for a cousin of mine, no one would have lifted their head. No one wanted to be named after a god, having briskly understood no such thing exists. Had I come by, what kind of emotion would I have seen in their eyes? None. Doesn't hunger make people blind? None, not even fear. Did they hold hands? Anybody? Not sure. Did anyone sing?

THE NAME

L osing him wasn't a fear or a feeling.

It was something else, a razor edge I walked on, a tightrope stretched over a chasm, a bridge swinging in the wind. More vertigo than panic. Like a hidden wound invisibly pouring blood in my lungs, and yet without smothering me. Rather, like a fact of nature.

Of history, it turned out. Or prehistory. I remembered, when my son turned eighteen.

I recalled. Nineteen twenty-six, and she was twenty-four. She had my name and last name, or the other way around, if you like. And the baby, one-month-old, had my baby's name. Don't ask me who came first.

They were on the boat, the boat on the ocean. Can you be more stranded, more lost? The two of them. She was twenty-four and she wore a black skirt, ankle length, a black blouse, a shawl. A scarf on her head, her hair braided. She had never left her small village. She didn't read or write.

No, the husband hadn't seen the baby. The husband was in America. They were going, now. Don't ask her how long it will take. She knows not, can't even imagine. She's afraid but she doesn't feel it. Fear is not an emotion. It's a rope bridge swinging right and left in the wind. It is nausea of the heart and soul, not only of the guts.

Then, the baby gets pale. Then the baby stops moving and makes no more sounds. The poor thing, one month old.

There's a doctor aboard. There must be. Someone's taking the baby from her arms. She is twisting her hands and clenching her teeth. She can't utter a word. Something's tightening up in her throat. The blueness is blinding.

Maybe a minute has passed. They have put the baby in a whitish bag, made of cloth, a miniature shroud.

Baby is dead. They are going to throw him overboard, as usual. They are not going to keep a corpse for a month. There are no fridges on immigrant ships. Not in the nineteen twenties. Not on those ships.

They are throwing my one-month-old father overboard, on his way to America. Finally, something breaks the dams in Grandmother's throat. Grandma, who bears my name, now screams like a slaughtered pig, like a fury. Grandma vomits her lungs on that damned deck, in the middle of ocean nowhere.

She runs forwards, she snatches the bag from the arms of whoever is bound to perform the rite. No, the funeral is not going to be.

"If you throw him I'll throw myself, if you throw him I'll jump," she yells. She holds the bundle against her breast like a Roman she-wolf would her Romolo.

And the baby slowly revives. Mistake? Miracle.

She will hang a St. Anthony medal around his neck. He will never take it off.

She could not lose him. Couldn't lose my father, Dad, her son who bears my son's name.

She could not.

Don't ask me. Don't ask me.

FERRYBOAT

I am enthralled by moments of passage, discontinuity. Someone dies. Someone else is born. Someone first kisses or penetrates someone else. The crash of an accident. The takeoff of a plane.

Thinking of transportation, I get close to the fracture line that captured me first—two limbs of land facing and the ferry, its loud sirens signaling it's time to leave. Move away! The gates lock like a guillotine and everything goes dark. Close your eyes! You are in the belly of the whale. Billions, zillions of butterflies are fluttering inside your throat, while the smell of fish makes you dizzy.

Awkwardly, the ship eases its mass and then, smooth like an iron, slides over the blue. Oily waves shush against its flanks, molten velvet murmuring secrets, lulling you to sleep. Wake up! The other side already towers afore, gulping you with its mighty jaw. With a shock, a punch in your gut, the ferry meets the opposite shore. The wide gate shrieks open. People tumble out like pebbles, garish, colorful, small. They step onto the continent. Back to the island. Farewell. Welcome. Farewell.

And a nameless chasm in between.

LIKE A TRAIN

The train took about fourteen hours from Rome to Messina if everything went well, that was kind of hard to predict. Fourteen hours were a good bet, a reasonable expectation.

Certainly they didn't seem long to me. Actually they established a kind of permanent pattern. My commutes routinely hit the same mark in the following decades... on airplanes though, crossing over oceans and continents, not just twisting and twirling down the peninsula, railroad squeezed between mountains and shore.

The train going from Rome to Messina didn't know of straight lines, quick diagonals, direct, easy solutions. Not a bit. But how can I tell you how I enjoyed the Odyssey, delays and detours notwithstanding? How I savored every nook and cranny of the Mediterranean coast, each town, suburb, periphery, hamlet fully acknowledged through endless wait for no passenger.

Those breaks also occurred in the middle of nowhere, for no apparent reason besides studying an iron gate's fancy curls, or a jasmine bush lacing an anonymous wall... a few tomato plants attached to their stakes, fruit ripe, almost at reach, though there would have been time to descend and buy a basketful. As there would have been time to list long rows of laundry hung to dry between windows, reconstructing age, gender and occupations of all the clothes' owners.

Machinists knew how to smell the roses by then. Those train travels were an inexhaustible source of stimuli, widening one's map of reality as well as boosting the flights of one's imagination, should boredom momentarily kick in. But, you see, we weren't going to Milan. No business meeting expected anyone in Messina or in any of the countless in-between stations. If a business meeting had improbably existed, it would have waited.

*

On my way South I was as happy as a lark, journeying towards what to me was a paradise of perpetual summer, a holiday of the soul. On my way North, back to my parents and school, I might have been less peppy, though the ride still brought joy and the ineffable thrill of transit. That unique, irreplaceable status.

The train going from Rome to Messina and vice versa is where I truly belonged and I'll tell you why. During those fourteen hours of permutation I was technically no one, as in order to be somebody you must be somewhere, correct? At a precise moment in time. Well, there are exceptions, I know, but I said "body." Ghosts and similar escape the rule. I am not talking of them.

When the train is huffing and puffing and you are aboard, identity eludes you. You can hardly be defined, as you will have vanished before a formulation was made. You cannot be pinned down as long as you keep moving.

On the train, my eyes drinking whatever the window pours in, I am a dot like these slipping-by houses, like these telegraph poles. Pixelation, that's all. I enormously like it. It gives me the exhilaration of freedom. I don't think God can see me. Not now.

*

My schoolmates in Rome call me *terún*, a nickname applied to the Southerner, namely to Sicilians. Demeaning, of course, but I still don't understand the nuance. It means brown, the color of earth. It means dirty with earth. It means soil-ed.

I have the slightest of accents. Sometimes a drawl escapes me and I can't control it. Should I? Cousins of mine were sent to French school at an early age to correct their diction, forcing on their tongue, so to speak, an opposite twist, narrow, nasal. The result is the most disconcerting hybrid, signaling them as oddities, making them a true laughing stock.

My parents haven't imposed such torture on my siblings or me. We have kept the hint of an accent. A shade, but it is sufficient to earn me the despicable *terún* label. I am not upset, as I don't truly grasp the humiliating connotation (humus=dirt). But I understand the key point: though I am in Rome, I am not Roman like the rest of my mates. Am I different? This is also too vague a concept.

I am not one of them, my mates think. This is clear. This comes through. Cuts through. I'll tell you how it feels. Slightly cold. A bit chilly. It makes you want to swallow, simultaneously tying a knot in your throat. It makes you want to look at your feet, but you don't. You only look on the side. There's an itch you get, regarding yourself. You are not sure you like yourself very much. Not entirely. You would like to scratch, get a ripple of blood under your fingernails. Tiny, just to calm the darn itch.

But you are also tempted to be proud. To smile, flashing your teeth, as if you had been paid a compliment. For you are kind of special, are you? You can be talked about. You have your peculiarity, dear *terún*… You have been discovered. Dug out. Brought into the sunlight, though you still feel damp. Humid. Humiliated.

*

When I am in Messina with my grand folks, feeling nurtured, rooted, ready to yell: "Moment, stop, you are beautiful!" (losing my soul to Satan, but who cares), relatives I am brought to for showing and greeting invariably exclaim: "Here comes the little Roman! How's our *Romanina* today?" I smile. What can I do? I am not fully realizing what's implied by these utterances. I can't put it in words, but I sense it and it is unpleasant. The corners of my mouth pull and hurt.

These folks are mocking me out of envy. They know people from the continent, especially from the capital city, feel superior to Southerners, especially islanders. So they softly ironize about my supposed airs. They assume I'd look down at them and they outsmart me, preventively enthroning me of their own will. Our dear little princess… How are things at the palace? Do you sleep in silk sheets? Did you have lunch with the Pope? With the President?

I have no clue about what they mean. I would like to cry. I am not Roman! Oh dear! Isn't it where you just came from? Be it then. I am if you say so. Is it that bad? You can't talk our dialect, they say. You don't understand this or that word.

But I perfectly do, having spent half of my life in Messina. Half is not enough, sweetheart. In fact it is a terrible quantity. Horrifyingly ambiguous. The ending line… they aren't being mean. They only state I am not

39

one of them. I have already experienced this strange, aching temblor.

*

On the train I ponder the philosophical contradiction I have chanced upon. Shit! I am not this, I am not that either. They all say so. What *I* say doesn't matter. They know better because they *are* the thing in question. Hundred per cent.

Now, what kind of option is left in my case? Being two things can be confusing but feasible. Let's say both Sicilians and Romans were claiming me. "You are one of us, darling!" Then again: "You belong here, don't you?" I could agree with these and with those in different instances. I should then separately allay feelings of betrayal, maybe unspool a multiple-personality syndrome. But I'd know they all want me and accept me.

Love me? So I would hope. While the actual case is no one does. I am not this, they swear, I am not that. Neither this nor that. True, the repudiation occurs in distinct places, and both groups are unaware of what happens on the other end. I could profit of such decalage. I could not tell *terúns* that Romans don't want me in their rows, and the other way around. Wisely, I don't.

But alas I am aware of the shameful truth. Let me put it straight: it isn't a matter of entity, essence, however you want to call it. It is not that, being neither one thing nor its opposite, I cease being. This conundrum is not menacing my existence. Here I am. I breathe, think, feel, sense, see. Hell I do. The discomfort only pertains to inclusion, meaning love.

What did I just say? Am I kidding? Can't people also love strangers? They can't. Am I going to be loved in this life? Forget it.

*

I have figured this at an early age, while I bounced like a tennis ball between island and mainland, between parents and grand folks, schoolmates and homeschooling. I have espoused my status of rarity, "thing-that-comes-from-elsewhere" wherever she stands. Therefore I don't stand. I run. I feel happy on the train that belongs nowhere.

Actually this particular train, in the nineteen sixties and seventies, belongs everywhere, as I was saying. It trots along the Apennines with the nonchalance of a slug. It allows me to absorb in detail myriads of possibilities, thousands facets of life's virtuality. It shows me what I could become, should I choose to impromptu alight in this particular hamlet. With the jasmine, tomatoes, ornate iron gate.

Zillions of opportunities are open to the stranger. You can be a stranger anywhere, while you only belong somewhere if others agree. Like the train, I understood I would be a trajectory. Watching at the landscape from this window, station to station to station. Like a train I would be a moving point of view. Passing house. Telegraph pole. Pixelation.

RUMOR

What brings back this obsolete memory on the day of your son's funeral? Your young son, aged 55 while you are 91. What prompts you to go back three quarters of a century and revive those minutes, those hours, with such iconic vividness?

As you open your mouth, your words aren't uttered but inscribed, rather etched in stone than just aired. Their perfection, adhesion to meaning, polished economy give them substance, make them tridimensional. Doubtlessly, your terse lines belong to the eternal domain like the recitation of bards, those who didn't have to piece a story together as if sewing a garment. They delivered it whole, alive like a baby.

Why instead of talking of your deceased progeny, of articulating your pain, are you choosing to report a fact buried in the past? How relevant can it be to your present plight?

Slowly, I recognize a tale I have heard long ago, perhaps in early childhood. An impression of familiarity surfaces. These sentences of yours have already carved a mark in my soul, left an imprint, created a small niche. I have forgotten them but they have modified me. On the day of my sibling's funeral I'm glad to reacquaint them. They soothe me, not sure how.

As you opened the window, that morning, you spotted the plane. Right in front of you and not unusual a sight, yet something struck you as strange. The perception didn't reach your consciousness but it caused you to suspend your breath, senses alerted. The plane was much lower than usual, and looked perfectly still. Then you noticed the small rectangular portal. As you stared, it slid open. Then you saw the bomb.

You run downstairs yelling at your mother, your sisters. They were still in their nightgowns. They threw shawls on their shoulders although it was summer. Just a reflex of decency, an instinct, no time was there for rational thoughts. And where was your father? Fighting at some remote northern front, you explain. Far, your father was far.

You describe a panicked crowd rushing toward the countryside, too distressed even to keep count of itself. People stared at the dusty road, trying to leave the urban center as rapidly as possible, seeking abode among hills and forests, lost to the enemy's eye.

You recall the farm where you hid with your mom, young sisters and brothers. I forget the name of the place as soon as you enounce it, busy picturing you, thin, dark, seventeen in nineteen forty-three, on the twelfth day of August. From your abode you listened to the dense, restless, ominous din of the bombs.

Later, taking advantage of your mom's distracted exhaustion, you sneaked away.

How did you dare? You felt a compulsion, you say, to come back to the house, which was in the very center of town. Your eyes anxiously rose to the window of the room that only contained your bed, and a shelf where half a dozen books were lined up. Had contained. All was destroyed by now.

The room where, thanks to unjustified favoritism, thanks to your mother's weakness, you had the privilege of sleeping alone, was no more than a walk-in closet. A small cot was pushed against the adobe wall. The shelf was a plank of wood. The books, we said, half a dozen. Yet you immensely cared for that sanctuary, those volumes. They were your entire world, so you had to return. No risk seemed excessive.

You looked up. Hope always dies last. All had been pulverized.

But you weren't done. Your dad's workshop was next. It was on the main square and you rushed in that direction, your feet moving faster than your brain. As you turned the corner, the glare made you stagger. The quasi absence of shadow made light change of status, become thicker and sharper, grow untamed. Gutted out, the square seemed unlimited. Suddenly your knees mollified. You feared you might be unable to cross, as if in front of you weren't a flat expanse of concrete but the ocean, deep, treacherous.

Yet you made it.

By a miracle, which did not relieve you at the moment (you registered it in a mechanical way, leaving feelings for later) the boutique was still standing. Inside, all was dark and silent, also orderly, intact.

Only as you stepped out you realized the door was unlocked. Hadn't you just entered it? Yes, but in a dream, in a trance. In fact, it was stuck open and you needed closing it. The impulse was mandatory, irresistible. You got hold of a hammer, began hitting the jamb to realign whatever had been twisted out of place. Each blow echoed so loud it chilled the blood in your veins, amplified by the uncanny emptiness around you. After each blow you paused, your forearm shaking, your throat tightening. Then, you hit once more.

As you stopped your racket, having finally shut the door behind you, you noticed the other noise, unmistakable. Still subdued but gaining momentum, the obnoxious buzz of a giant insect. An aircraft was patrolling, ugly bird of death circling, ready to shoot at whatever moved underneath. But you needed to leave the plaza, the town, go back to the hiding place. You had to calculate that vulture's speed and trajectory, then slip between its claws. How long did it take for you to traverse the square? You know it seemed infinite. You had to identify each possible cover amidst such desolation. They were spare. A residue of marble bench. The carcass of a car. You had to dash, madly running, your body compressed in a fist, an arrow, a vector. Bundle up, wait for the thing to fly past. In the meanwhile you studied your next shelter, ready to leap again.

When, later, you reported the news to your mom (no house but Dad's workshop still up, in good order, even locked against looters) she got furious. How did you…?

Three quarters of a century later I can tell you don't have a plausible answer. What's the point, today, Father, of recalling that morning, that blinding light? Today is overcast and drizzling. It's a bleak winter day and bells are tolling. They are calling to your son's funeral mass. The crowd flowing through the square wears black. They have winter coats, scarves. The square is another one, in another town. I concede it is wide and also looks ominous. It looks huge, impassable, a treacherous stretch of water. And the coffin sliding forth is a creepy gondola, a thick-skinned cetaceous of sorts, mute and indecipherable.

Do you wonder about death, how it turned above you back then, round and round, blind, inexorable? And it missed you, and you fooled it but what for since it caught you in the end? It caught you by treason, by ruse, by mistake, in the flesh of your progeny.

I don't know if this is what occupies your mind. Did you come back to your bombed town, that morning, to unlid a coffin of sorts, unbury a mean secret, unwilling to accept ignorance, bound to confront the truth as scary as it might be? Perhaps.

As you paint the story of that day you sit in a battered armchair, in your studio lined up with myriads of volumes. Walls of volumes, a whole house made of printed pages within which you have cocooned for a lifetime. As if that half dozen the bomb devoured were a seed that could only germinate, producing a forest, this forest. Today what is this forest worth? I suspect you might be asking yourself this very question.

I suspect you might be pondering survival, and its qualities. Its ambiguous appeal and strange brilliance. Its uncanny noise, unbearable loneliness.

DEAD BROTHER

Only haven amidst the vortex of grief, this small graveyard and its minute, strange coziness. Forlorn, lost in the middle of nowhere, niched inside a depression of the grounds, practically invisible. Blind, rather blindfolded, high walls block its entire perimeter, obstructing the view.

The monotonous row of miniature temples, all the same, dull, unpretentious, look like students of an old country school, bored yet disciplined. No superfluous adornment is in view. On the contrary, abandoned tools, unkempt trails and flowerbeds emanate an aura of shabbiness. Logs, twigs, branches piled in a corner hint ironically at a hypothetical bonfire. Pine trees spill their needles together with cute wooden balls, toy-like and distracting.

Noisy, lengthy, laborious, a mason seals with bricks and mortar the burial cell.

Matrix. Womb. Obstructing and smothering. Blind, blindfolded.

Laying bricks is pragmatic, efficient, therefore un-ceremonial. It takes skills, not mannerisms. As I look, routine, repetition seeps into my veins, summoning back life and its forward motion, relentless. Bricks like minutes, like hours, like days. Rows of bricks like months, years—now, none of your business.

The surrounding landscape only appears if I retrace my steps, pass the cast-iron gate, reach the parking lot. On the right, stairs lead to a small chapel, a bare cube of stone, crumbling, desolate. The front door is closed. I peek through the keyhole. I see darkness.

The retaining wall of the stairs is a perfect perch. This slight elevation allows a hint of perspective, a breath of fresh air. Saddled over the edge, legs dangling, I feel something raw, something raven dilating my lungs.

Brambles line the road on both sides. Tiny meadows shyly punctuate the view. Wide, rounded, benevolent crowns of conifers float between earth and sky. The meek voice of sheep ripples through the evening calm, together with a lulling sound of cowbells.

A large dog, so kin to the fellow beasts it protects—same size, same whitish fleece, their soft, gentle guardian—turns a corner, comes forwards. Here's the shepherd spying at the passing vehicles, promptly herding his flock, squeezing it against prickly borders. Soon he resumes his progress, leading his cortege towards the graveyard, as if aiming for good at this sweet enclave, no larger than a pen.

Modest, scarce, the mob is complete. A black sheep beautifully contrasts its mates' dusty pallor, muzzle hitting barbed wire, body askew. You see, nothing is missing. Only shifting a bit, too fast probably.

Sound of bells, bleats (sad? hungry? alarmed?), rhythmic rasp of shovels splattering then spreading lime, heavy thumps of bricks falling in place, obedient and rigorous, try to harmonize as if this all made sense. They remain slightly off tune. I wonder if you'd be disturbed. If you'd choose to be lenient. If you would forgive.

DYNASTY

As we visit the place of origin, I desperately look for a bathroom. The house has many, but all have some kind of impediment— missing lock, broken window sending in a chill draft, run out toilet paper. This one, which looks pristine, is Father's, therefore inaccessible. As I finally pick whatever is closer, Mom sneaks in, eager for a bit of conversation. Mother, not while I pee. I am an adult. I have the right to decide in front of whom I'd take my pants off, and it isn't you. I can't say this, of course, though sometimes I have yelled it in her face out of exasperation. She was shocked, incapable of making sense of what seemed like gratuitous cruelty or a weird overreaction. Why shouldn't she see me bare-assed, taking a leak, while she tells me about a silk blouse she just bought? I am flesh of her flesh, blood of her blood, she pleads. I would like to reply I was, long ago. Not any more. All of our body cells die sooner or later and fresh ones substitute them. At some point we are entirely new. I have long ceased belonging to you, Mom. Of course, her counterargument is solid, made of steel. Jesuitic as she is, subtler than a defense lawyer, she says new cells are born by the previous ones. See? Whatever I am or become is just a byproduct of the original stuff. I, in other terms, have no way of cutting the bond be- tween us, from now to eternity. So she claims, unaware of the fact her theory implies a huge, unbroken tapestry, as her cells are her mother's and so forth. Then if it all belongs, Mother, nothing does. Or else, to determine who is whose becomes problematic. Let go of your pretense. Leave this restroom alone, will you? Never mind. I am done.

God! The bedroom Mom fixed for me and my son is tiny. Mother always went for miniature beds, Snow White style, I mean like those the Seven Dwarves slept in. True, we were a large family and space wasn't abundant. The undersized cots Mother fancied were bunk-able, little towers we loved to escalate. But now many of them have been piled, storage-fashion, in the dusty recess we were assigned for the night. Mother, your hospitality, just as your domesticity, always had a fabulous twist. This room comes straight out of a fairy tale. All the beds have been made, sheets pulled tight, stark white like the pages of a virgin notebook. Slightly askew… the frames are imperfectly stacked, perhaps broken or bent. Will this hazardous scaffolding hold? Flowers are tucked in each bed, fresh and bright, head displayed on the pillow, stem hidden under ironed linen. Are they a decoration? On the surreal side. Suddenly I recall Little Ida, one of Hans Christian Andersen's girls. Didn't she put her flowers in bed as if they were dolls? In a drawer, I guess. Mom gave me her own copy of Andersen's tales, a thick volume bound in brown cloth. It looked like a box. A suitcase? Drawer chest. Closet. Room? Dollhouse. Now these beds, like white pages inscribed with floral hieroglyphs... What are we supposed… what kind of dreams… nightmares… Mom, we will sleep like angels.

Early the morning after we are leaving. Stop in New York City. The town is airy, tall, cool, transparent. As we go for a leisurely stroll, close to sunset, shades of pink tint the sky then spill everywhere, refracted by a zillion windows, glass panes, shiny walls. How have I found myself in this humongous square where an art performance takes place? Yes, a kind of happening. As if we were still in the nineteen eighties, audience participation is sought. I don't usually fancy this kind of games, but today I am in a whimsical mood. Maybe I'll play along. We are asked to volunteer descent in a manhole situated within the pedestrian area. Safe enough. I have never been scared of viscera. Moreover, I have always been an outsider… will this plunge make an insider of me? Maybe if I tuck in long enough. Just a few steps down a ladder embedded into the wall, a small ledge sticks out of the concrete. This is where I shall sit, my head at ground level. Easy? Sure. Still, it is vertiginous. My perspective has entirely changed. How weird is the world from down here. The sky so remote, and simultaneously incumbent. The light… I need a smoke. Here, with a cig hanging from my beak I feel less awkward. Wiser, prone to reflection. In this cradle of calm, concealed, forgotten (what are they doing up there? strange, how this slight gap isolates me, muffling all sounds) I think of heaven and hell. Mmmmh, I'm sure they have figured it wrong as far as logistics go. Heaven must be deep and low, for the sake of laying flat on your back and looking up, right? Look at the light that wanders, escapes, explodes, flies.

Immaterial and yet unbearably beautiful, light has such an effect on me—fulfilling, then going the extra measure. Spilling, like bliss does. Trespassing. Once, long time ago, Mother asked me to list all the things I most loved. She had those out of the blue "teacher" moments. She'd dare you with an educational task for the sake of it. Why that question, though? What was she possibly thinking? I was a grown-up, long gone. Did she sense I was sad? Melancholic? Well, I was obedient. That same night I opened my journal and wrote. Item number one, no doubt, was the smell of bread. I lived on top of a bakery. Not a good one. They made sandwiches by the ton for some institution, prison, hospital. Drab, semi-industrial stuff. The smell was divine nevertheless. At dawn, it climbed all the way from the basement to the seventh floor where I dwelled in the servants' quarters. Enough for me to jump out of bed, ready to live another day and quite hungrily. Item number two was light, no further defined. Yes, light made me happy. Still does.

Did I send my list back to Mom? I believe I didn't. She used to forget her requests as soon as she formulated them. Had she still remembered this one, she'd promptly forget my answers. Wasn't it bizarre, anyway, such pretense at therapy of hers? Paradoxical. Did she even suspect that if her child had a bent for sadness, she might hold some responsibility indeed? Wasn't that your knife, Mom, stuck into my side? Wasn't it your hand distractedly pushing? With the other hand you often brandished a wad of cotton, soft and fluffy, imbibed with iodine. I have seen you doing it on many an occasion, a wink on your face, eyebrow lifted with innuendo. Fine, but wouldn't it have been easier to pull the knife out?

Now we sit under a bridge, Brothers, Sister and I, still in the Big Apple. Evening has come and I have climbed out of my hole, though I can't exactly remember how and when. We have reunited for dinner, the four of us, like when we were kids. We clump in tight formation. On our right is a pyramid of discarded pizza boxes. On our left a pile of dirt white, something powdery and crumbly. It is parmesan cheese, I reckon, gone bad. Who would toss such a quantity? It must have been poisonous. How appropriate for Wops to end up in such company.

Notice how we are sitting... in a square, facing out, back rested against back. Don't we look like some kind of pizza-in-a-box? Maybe not. The analogy comes to me out of exhaustion, and some sense of dejection. How did we get this low? By the way, didn't I just say that's where heaven lies?

Do you still remember, I mumble while I munch on, when Dad came to New York for the first time? He didn't speak a word of English. On his way to the Metro station he was lost, and embarrassed because he couldn't ask for directions. That bad, Daddy? Then he saw two guys digging a trench. Inside the trench, actually. Struck by a sudden inspiration he squatted, smiled, then he addressed them in his hometown dialect. They replied without lifting their eyes, spade in hand. How happy was he of his cleverness! How proud, when he related the episode! Proud of what, Papa, exactly? Of knowing that your co-nationals (your co-villagers) necessarily would be doing dirt work? Did you feel what I felt when I cocooned in the manhole, that if you dive into the guts of the city you become an insider? You don't.

Yet I cling to this story of Dad's. It fills me with tenderness. It reminds of me of a legend of where I come from, a story I am fond of but I don't know why. It's the myth of a fisherman who was sent under the sea by the king, to check the island's foundations. Are they, His Majesty asked, appropriately bolted? Earthquakes struck the area quite regularly. Colapesce (that is the name of the fisherman) made his careful round. Bad news. The island rests on three pillars, Sire. Two are fine, but the third is broken. Then do something, Cola, or else we'll be sinking. Yes, My Lord. Cola bravely plunged (no one could resist underwater as long as he did). He hugged the pillar, held it tight, carrying the weight of the world (one third of the island) on his shoulders. He's still there, now become a legend. Talk about a careless ruler. About a patient subject. True supporter. Why am I enthralled with this pathetic tale? I don't know. Such bloody melancholy.

We are having dinner, Brothers, Sister and I. Our position, undoubtedly good for our vertebras, doesn't help conversation. As we squat, knees close to our chest, don't we look like dice? Like cubes in a box, those toy sets in favor during our childhood. Now they are so obsolete that you only can find them in antique stores, quite worn, mostly incomplete. Those cubes, puzzled together, made a story. They composed a scene, I mean, from a fairy tale. There are six sides to a cube, each belonging to a different narrative. Therefore the box contains six stories, all scrambled, unless you find the matching sides of all cubes. Which you don't, because it takes patience and you get tired, bored, your sibling interrupts you. The game isn't age appropriate. Cubes roll under the bed. They get lost. They are used like weapons. They are quite heavy and have corners. The game should be taken off the market, where indeed it has ended. Still, it's coming to mind, now. Don't we look like those dice?

The whole family, I mean, Mom and Dad included. Six of us, each one side of the cube, facing outward and unable to see the other five. Being all on a same plane is actually impossible. We cannot coexist. Can't (should not) belong to the same story, of course. Truly, we have no idea of what the other stories are about. We don't communicate, although we are as intimate as it can be. Try to take off a side from a cube. The entire thing collapses. We share corners. We share long thin edges, each of us with four mates, rubbing, elbowing, scratching. As for our direct opposite, we are allowed to ignore it. I don't know who mine is... identities are flexible. I know little of my neighbors as well, though we are close and we tumble, incessantly gasping for air, trying in turns to reach the surface, the top, heaven, that famous place in the sun... Wait. Is it my own family? Is it us? What about the other cubes? Where did the box go?

I just mentioned it. There's a pile of filthy old pizza containers, leaned against one of the pillars holding the bridge. What a perfect place for a Dagos' reunion. But we are not eating pizza. Truly, we can't stand the smell of it, the acrid pungency of undercooked tomato sauce. As if the world didn't know how long and amorously juices need to simmer before they get tame, lose their wilderness.

SALT OF THE EARTH

The nuns' pasta had a wide reputation, and consistently bad. It was actually a term of comparison used to point at terrible cooking.

Why pasta of all food? In our country it wasn't a course but a symbol. Always present (a twice-daily entrée) its success depended on timing and care rather than ingredients. Pasta was only good if cooked just as long as needed in sufficient, full boiling, properly salted water. Drained and seasoned in a blink then, with firm, expert gestures. Hesitation would be fatal, delay catastrophic. All prospective eaters should be fork in hand, as the cook vivaciously scooped away.

Therefore, pasta meant domestic efficiency and love.

Its seasoning added to the concept. Being usually a simple tomato sauce, its appeal hid in minor details each cook claimed to master. Not all tomato sauces were the same, cooks suggested with a tone of conspiracy. Due to mysterious tricks and slight, secret adjustments, pasta condiments ranged from exquisite to frankly disgusting, which defines the nuns' tomato sauce.

I have abundantly sampled it when allowed to stay in school for the afternoon. Having lunch at the nunnery where I attended elementary was fun. It provided me with a thrill of freedom, due to the long absence from home. The meal's quality was the least of my worries. I would have gulped stones without noticing.

But I can reconstruct consistency and flavor of the *pastasciutta* we ate. First of all it wasn't dry, as its name implied and tradition exacted. It was wet. The sauce, too thinned out, mollified the noodles, giving them a gummy texture and a tendency to stick together. They were usually insipid. And cold, tepid at best. Their bloody red condiment had the slight acidity of canned juice insufficiently labored by the magic of mothers, aunties, grandmothers.

Pasta felt overcooked. It probably wasn't. It became it by the time it left those tall, towering pots to reach hundreds of plastic bowls (one more tasteless touch).

Catholic schools weren't fancy places by then in my country, but a cheap form of education. They were crowded. Kids of working class often remained after noon, though lessons were uniquely taught in the morning. But their folks couldn't afford nannies. Older siblings were already employed and if grandparents had died or, as it commonly occurred, still lived in the village, nuns would be the default.

They organized naive (yet no less delightful) after-school activities such as choir singing, craft making, ball games in the courtyards and, of course, helping out. This last happened to be the most interesting. Helping anywhere, including those giant, imposing, quasi-industrial kitchens that I came to know well. In their womb I acquired a taste for community. I found comfort in their plain essentiality, their safe anonymity. I had never enjoyed complex rituals around food... they loaded something natural with an artificial surplus, indigestible.

To me the nuns' pasta was good. When I gulped it, I was hungry from exertion and fun, hurried to fill up and then run towards more exertion and fun.

*

She came in as a substitute when I was in eight grade. Our literature and language instructor (who taught several subjects, being responsible for the class overall preparedness) had left without warning at midyear. She had a nervous breakdown, we were told. It sounded scary and vague. She was questioning her religious vocation and she might leave the congregation. It sounded gossipy, though not unheard of. It recurrently occurred.

Being dumped so briskly was bad. We had exams to prepare. Graduation was close. Our principal needed to find someone strong and competent... not too much of a disciplinarian, we hoped. We couldn't help worrying.

She was unbelievably small, a child size, a miniature. Old by our standards, which could be anything over forty. Of course we couldn't judge by her hair, sealed under the veil. But a grayish mustache shaded her upper lip, conferring authority. Not that we would doubt such a quality. Sister Mia was a powerhouse. She could have handled a regiment instead of a bunch of teens and I wonder if she actually did, at least once. I would not be surprised.

In a blink she assessed our scholastic weaknesses (our previous teacher had slackened before quitting) and perfected her plan of attack. We would all pass the exams with top grades, she announced and we shivered, afraid of being overburdened. But we shouldn't have. She was as inflexible as fair. We had to do what she asked for, which was reasonable although didn't admit excuse. We should comply, period. Once done, we were done.

I liked her right away. A fact of chemistry… is it possible between kids and old nuns? I think so. She had come back from Spain where she was sent during the Civil War, then allowed to indefinitely stay. Did they summon her for our sake? She liked it best there, she admitted. During the Civil War, paradoxically, she had become a Communist. She had seen social injustice too closely, she explained, for not taking a definite stance.

We believed voting Communist was forbidden to Catholic nuns. It was perfectly fine, she affirmed, her mustache, pearled with minuscule beads of sweat, fiercely quivering.

*

I was a trouble girl at the time. After elementary I was switched from the bad-pasta-school to a more snobbish institute and I hadn't been able to adjust. Disconnected from my schoolmates, all belonging to higher social ranks, I resented my difference. I was bored by study and eager for something I missed, without having a clue of what it might be.

Sister Mia sensed my unrest. She had perfectly pinpointed each student, firmly holding the group in her palm. She proposed me a deal. She would spare me a few hours of class in exchange for some extra homework. I was quick to accept. She exacted a translation from Latin each morning, a full page she delivered as soon as she saw me, then asked for the day after. For six months I complied. It was hard, but then it got easier. Soon enough I could do the job in less than an hour. Then I started to enjoy it like a game, a charade I craved to unspool. I did not miss a day.

Afterwards, I had changed, I was someone else. I'm aware of it now, though I still can't explain what happened.

My reward. At mid morning, when language courses were over and the class switched to lighter instruction, I was out. Sister Mia drove her Fiat 600 as I sat at her side, having loaded the vehicle with stuff of all sorts, food, books, toys, shoes, clothes. We crossed town heading towards a far and drab outskirt, so poor it seemed stuck back in time. Even in dry weather the terrain was muddy, probably for some sewer system fault, confirmed by the nasty smells. Vegetation was scanty and sad in spite of the soil moisture. Housing consisted in huts and barracks too sparse to be called a slum. In a cube of concrete of uncertain function, Mia had made her own alternative school. Obviously an only room, though we built dividers to allow various activities. I said we built, as I helped with any task my boss indicated.

As you guessed, I was thrilled to saunter from this to that, awed by each skill I discovered, masonry to electricity to plumbing to carpentry. But my duties weren't limited to construction. Sister Mia put my literacy at fruition… she wouldn't waste a drop of any resource at hand. She dispatched me from table to table in order to instruct the students in whatever subject I could even barely fake.

I was suddenly exposed to an unexpected model of operating: everyone was in charge, offering the level of skill she currently owned. All the way from elders to babies, these last always crowding the room that of course doubled as a nursery. Doubling is a limited word for the multi-functionality of what now would be called a cultural center, perhaps. Then, such term didn't exist. We just went with "school."

But how different was this school from the place where I was sent each morning, Latin version in hand. I loved this just as much as I loathed that. I am not sure of what my busy afternoons fulfilled. Many things, I suspect, and all paramount. Such as flexibility. Imagination. Generosity. Exchange. Equality.

Freedom.

Before hopping into the Fiat I changed in the restrooms, tossing into a plastic bag the blue uniform I hated. I wore what I believed most suited me, of course forbidden clothes, a tight-fitting blouse, bright green, and my favorite miniskirt. I wore hoses instead of socks and a pair of ballerinas replaced my moccasins. After all I might meet boys by leaving the convent, diving into Sister Mia's world, the real one. And she didn't care how I dressed. I looked pretty much like the girls I taught, like the sweet teen mothers whose kids I cuddled and fed while they learned their algebra and grammar.

Mia could teach it all, any level. I wouldn't have been able to judge the extent of her knowledge, and I sure didn't try. I was busy doing, busy enjoying. But I clearly recall that she could explain anything to anyone. I do not remember a time when she was at loss, were the problem a broken faucet or a calculus test. I don't know where she had acquired her diplomas, what she had studied or when. She was not in her prime, as proved by her graying mustache. Though her face, a small rosy apple, didn't bear many signs of wear. I knew nothing of her, but the present tense that wholly sufficed me. For I was in it, having fun.

*

In the morning I had made my snack more abundant, then halved it. My mom didn't realize it. She never figured out that at lunchtime I was inside a car, gladly riding with my beloved mentor. Almost every day I made my favorite sandwich, thickly buttered bread with a couple of anchovies. I felt almost guilty as I bit into that scrumptiousness, being spared both cafeteria and family meal. I adored the smell of fish and the salty tanginess, taste of ocean lingering on my tongue.

Freedom, did I call your name?

I never told a thing to my parents. Nothing, to nobody. I'm not sure about what the principal knew. The other teachers? While arrangements must have been made for my missing courses, they were never addressed in my presence. Grades on my report just remained the same, besides Latin, popped to a brave A+. For a dead language, it brought quite a life to my lousy teens.

June arrived, alas. We got our diplomas and quite brilliantly, as our sub had promised. Then we left for vacations while our folks chose the appropriate high schools. I remained in the same institute two more years, for gymnasium, at my great discontent. All my disquiet resumed.

Teachers obviously had changed and, alas, in the fall Mia wasn't around. Or I'm sure that we would have struck a deal, though I was no more of her students. But she was nowhere to be found. Rumors said she was sent back to Spain. Did she ask to? That would have been sad, almost cruel and yet understandable. She had been honest. She disliked our snobbish little society, even only part time. Did she follow orders? Nuns have to, even when they possess a mind of their own. Was she punished for something she did?

Was she, god forbid?

TRAVELERS

He brings a whole cucumber to the dinner table, sets it to the left of his plate. Does he need a small cutting board, the lady of the house inquires. He doesn't. The suggestion surprises him. Maybe (for sure) he isn't used to a tablecloth that greenish spills could stain. Maybe (for sure) he is used to eat on metal, plastic, bare wood. He cuts thick slices with a large knife, chopping them with a snappy motion, rubbing them with salt then gobbling them in one bite, cleaning his palate between courses or before drinking wine. Where did he learn?

From his South American years (Brazil, then Argentina where two daughters were born) he still misses maté—yet another green thing, thick and muddy. He explains about it with longing, as if speaking of a dear friend he has lost. Maté is grass soaking at the bottom of a tall, narrow mug, a thin straw slowing down the sipping, stretching out the pleasure.

Then he talks of Africa, and the first thing he mentions is tea made with hibiscus flowers. In the North, the deserts where he extensively traveled, Grandpa always refreshed himself with cool, crimson karkadé. The intense red of the concoction, I see, perfectly complements the green of maté. Strange, mysterious symmetry... I catch it. It means something I do not understand.

He also gives us a terrifying tale of tropical flies entering human brains by the ear, eating up a tunnel then exiting by the nose, having in the meanwhile destroyed cerebral tissues. We are shaken, appalled. He laughs at our sissiness. Is it true?

Hard to say. Grandpa's Africa is as blurred as his South America, both magnetic, enthralling in their fabulous vagueness. Did he bring back from overseas his love for large birds? The raven, the cockatoos he feeds amorously, calling them with exotic first names.

*

When I traveled for work to Brazil in my thirties I went to a market, in Rio, where people sold hammocks, wooden artifacts, metal ware, farm machinery, produce and woven rugs. That fair, I understood, had been going on for a century at least. Very old, still unchanged, traditional, poor. Suddenly, I realized my grandfather must have been there weekend after weekend, selling his copperware. Things must have looked to him like they now looked to me. He must have smelled meat broiled on wood fire, as I did. Like me he must have danced the Forró, which means "for all," borrowing its name from English-speaking strangers. Colonizers. Invaders.

At his side, intimidated by such boisterous father yet reassured by the same loud boldness, would have been a child, thin and dark, afraid of the tall stiltwalkers during Carnival season, deafened by the shrilling drums of the samba. What does Father recall of Brazil? Nothing but a sense of terrified awe and a longing for coconut sweets.

When I lived in Brazil, in my thirties, sometimes I went for walks with a colleague who translated Strindberg from Swedish. "Have you been in Swede?" I asked once. "No," he answered. He had never been out of the country, certainly not overseas. "I haven't been in Swede," he muttered, "but they say it exists." I smiled. I could have said the same about Grandpa's remote, fabulous exiles until I took a plane and went to verify one of them, stunned at the beauty of the Pão de Açúcar, Copacabana, Ipanema. Yes, the world he described existed.

Did it? After I left I started doubting it. I remembered it, though the memory as years went by became both blurred and psychedelic. The hibiscus flowers (weren't they also in North Africa?) became bigger and redder, the lagoon more cobalt, the macumba and the capoeira wilder. Sometimes I thought they might be the fruit of my imagination, though they had been real once. Too briefly.

Grandpa, about you? What happens to a dear one when he's long gone? He becomes a kind of abstract painting, an old map from which all writing is blotted. And it fades into patches of color, muddy green, bloody red. Lovely, yet more and more undefined.

ARIADNE'S SONG

And you knitted for hours. By the window, because of your faint sight. "I can't stay without a piece of work in my hands," you said. In a plaintive tone, yet not querulous.

You were too old and weak by then to conceive your own project. Someone (daughters? daughters-in-law? any good-willing relative) should decide what you'd do. They should buy the yarn or the fabric, then you'd gladly give it a start. You would sit by the window, very quiet but happy, I believed. Sometimes frowning and fretting about a detail you couldn't get right. But that was a private concern… Sighs or softly muttered words (your head bent, gaze intent, your thick glasses one inch from the needles) weren't meant for the public.

If I interrupted you, asking for such and such with the abrupt energy of the youth, so opposed to your hypnotic tranquility, you just lifted your gaze and you answered. Once on a while you whispered: "Wait a moment, I am counting my rows." Or your stitches. You lost count. You murmured with a broken note in your voice: "Oh my, I have to start over," that you patiently did.

Patience. How many barrels of it did you have in stock? Were you born with such an oversized supply? I doubt it. Did you spin it out during those eternities spent in the sole company of needles? I guess so. Still I miss a good reason.

You completed a countless quantity of blankets, curtains, tablecloths, towels, sweaters, camisoles, jumpers, socks, gloves, hats, swimsuits, anything that could be knit or crocheted. You did it for your kids, grandkids, your extended family and friends, always, but especially after your children married and house chores wound down. You were left with lots of free time and you didn't like it. You wanted something in your hands.

Most of it you had learned from the nuns at the boarding house, having lost your mom at the age of two. Although you resented your dad for sending you there (your stepmother didn't want you around as a memory of her predecessor, her rival), with the nuns you spent the sweet years of your youth. Those that don't come back, so we try to get back to them (the story of Mohammed and the mountain). You found safety, calm, order, maybe even fairness at the boarding house.

And the nuns, those strange sexless girls, taught you to never, never keep your hands aimless (what would hands be tempted to do if they weren't always occupied?) The nuns taught you everything related to so-called "women's work," even finger knitting... While you memorized your lessons or practiced songs, while you sat in the courtyard during recess, your bare hands hatched miles and miles of delicate cord perfect for hemming clothes, bed sheets, drapes. Your indexes and thumbs knew their way. No need to look down, to pay attention.

"I can't stay without work in my hands," you begged in the morning. Someone gave you a project and you beamed with gratitude.

That you could do whatever was asked, no matter how difficult (struggling with your fading memory or with hieroglyphic instructions), that your finished products were marvels, immaculate, faultless, that until your late nineties, almost blind, you could make lace out of silk so thin, the result looked like filigree, no one really acknowledged.

You did not seem to care. You didn't care, truly. As we said, that was your hands only, pride and ego weren't involved. Ego, pride, did you possess them? Not sure. All those things you made went like water under a bridge. They anonymously rushed away and you didn't mind.

You had an artist eye. At the nuns' you had learned watercolor, oil painting, pyrography. I saw samples. You showed them to me with a quasi-joyful smile. Those activities didn't last, as they weren't suited to your wifely routine. Only the textile related tasks belonged and remained. You could do whatever your household required although, as you got older, knitting, crocheting, mending became predominant. Linear skills, requiring attention but a smaller and smaller focus. Circumscribed world, gathered on a microscope slide.

Didn't you get bored? Depressed?

Obsessed?

I believe that the thread secured you. I can feel it, now that I've reached the age you were when I was born. Now that I'm about to become you, I look for your gestures. Here they are. I lost nothing. It must be because of this thread I'm holding. It leads me all the way back.

Did the wool in your lap connect you to something, someone, your past, a root of sorts? Or did you just enjoy the softness? The warm suppleness rubbing against your fingertips, lightly brushing your forearms and wrists.

Isn't holding cloth like holding a human being? An ideal one. A lost one, but also a potential one. A quiet, harmless love vessel, a recipient for our lovemaking. Isn't lovingly making clothes just like making love? It is. Is baby-clothes-making like making babies? Yes, Grandma.

In the evening, before bed, you rolled your in-progress piece within a clean cloth. As professionals do because fabric is living matter, needs protection and care. On the cloth you left your glasses—your signature, the undeniable trace of your presence. I miss seeing that neat, precious bundle that meant you.

I have stolen a silver hook (double zero size) and a scrap of yarn from your bed stand after you passed away. I have kept them. I am alone as well, Grandma, and sometimes I have time on my hands, or else I can make it. I was born an orphan like you, in spite of my dear parents. I am an orphan at soul. I understand.

HOMESPUN

Her hair still strong enough, once solidly grabbed, tightly twisted, to make a decent rope. So intimately attached to her skull, she could hang over the edge of a ravine and not fall. She could be saved, she is sure, if someone took hold of her hair, quickly spiraled it into a coil and pulled up.

The roots, see—though if you look at the discolored tip of a single specimen, it's about a sixteenth of an inch long—aren't shallow. They dive in. They probe depths unfathomed.

She remembers how he has tried to extirpate it when she was a child, unripe, unexperienced. How he has sneaked into the deforesting process, slyly attacking a few strands at a time, often during the night. How he has grinned at his hands holding the stolen booty—a shattered cobweb.

But his ambuscades didn't leave marks. No bald patch. Just a little redness, a sting, memories of wounds invisible. Hair has a way to grow over, mix and match, masquerade.

And why did he wish to erode the proliferous bush, the wild little grove topping her head? She did not understand, busy escaping, as she felt a kind of responsibility towards that grove of hers, little copse entrusted to her care.

Hair mostly thrives on wind. Sometimes water. But this last can be forgone, truly, because hair feeds on sky, all kind, overcast or cloudless. Hair, no matter its shade, metabolizes blue, gray, cool green. It vibrates at the speed of outer atmospheres.

Yet such freedom, such affinity with things light, immaterial, only enforces hair's core quality of concrete sturdiness.

Should she fall, or be pushed, over a precipice, she could count on this extra limb, this appendix she has cultured against all odds. Like, let's say, a potted plant of rosemary, drying and resprouting in turns, she would carry from a rented room to the next. Amorously, window to window to window.

WISTERIA

Is it the profusion, the abundance of blooms? Or the elegant curve, the reclining arch? The unspeakable shade—blend of lilac and mauve, tenderly ambiguous, like a caressing hand, uncertain and burning. A shade of nostalgia, regret.

Why do I love wisteria? Is it because of esthetics? There is history too. The plant flooded with blossoms my grandparents' veranda, where we happily sat during summer nights.

There, at five, I saw a grown-up cry. A girlfriend of Mother, she wept for a thing strange and bad, a lost love. No idea of what it was, but it sounded painful like a shrilling note on the piano. I remember the lady's blond hair, hanging like straw over her face. Falling down like the wisteria surrounding us.

A year later perhaps, the trunk was cut to a stump. The roots were too powerful, threatening foundations and walls, Grandpa said. I was furious and hurt. I loved the wisteria. Could I have known the house itself would soon vanish (the land expropriated by the government for the most futile cause)? Could I have known Grandpa would be next, untimely erased by cancer? In a blink, annihilated, uprooted. What did I know of life and its cruelty? Nothing, but I liked the wisteria's mellow tears. They knew what I didn't, what it would take me decades to understand.

That life is a collapsing moment. Falling, and still stubbornly grasping stones, concrete, bricks for support. Frantic, seasonal, transient. Liquid, unforgettable. Lyrical, incomprehensible. Gone.

WOUNDED

Love is a mystery.

How it happens, even more how it doesn't. How it vanishes, and sometimes gets stuck. If it were a bird you'd wonder where it learned how to fly. Clearly, it would need more lessons.

It—we refer to an entity of sorts, independent, self-standing. But no such thing exists. Love is personal, like a body part. Like a tumor you develop on your own... that's why idiosyncrasy reigns. That is why we never agree when we talk about it. Each refers to his or her own. Tumor.

"I love you!" "You don't." "How can you be sure?" "You don't know what love means in the first place." Well, of course. We can only respond of our own. Tumor.

People would get mad should I publicly utter the above. Associate the word tumor with love, I mean. It has happened. I had even left "tumor" out, using the word "monster" instead. Sorry! But, first of all, I *love* monsters. They are usually cute. Secondly, I was using the term in its original meaning that is wondrous, amazing and strange, a combo of mismatched elements, a collage.

Or a crystal with a million facets, but we see the one facing us. Shiny, sometimes blurry. I could use the word crystal all right. No one would complain. I could use the words jewel, diamond. I won't.

When you'll come to the conclusion love doesn't exist if not for selling chocolates, rings, wedding gowns and the similar, you shall start calling your tumors scars. That takes the pressure off. Scars can be ugly, even awful, but they bulge less and are easier to hide. Sometimes they are discreet. They blend in, chameleon-like.

My first scar chisels my chest. All right, chronologically it isn't my first. For that I should go back to the Stone Age. You should too. The epidemic started early. We'll let go of ancient wounds. I meant first in anatomical order, starting at the top. Why? Why not.

It is afternoon, and everything I see is made of stone.

I am talking about the villa, his family country estate.

Well, the country in question is next door to town. They are contiguous. We drive a tiny bit and we arrive. At the same time we've gone very far, we have dug into feudalism, reached a quite remote past still drooling into the present, alas. His old family mansion… beware of those houses. They have too many secrets. As you pass the gate you feel danger. But it's late. You have been trapped.

We are not allowed in right away. It would be inappropriate. Indiscrete, as if the house were a lady, let's say, still disheveled. While she readies herself the maid will make tea, take out the *rosolio*. Meanwhile, we tour the gardens.

They are in state of abandon, he apologizes. Oh, dear… the condition immediately spreads. Is he attained? I am. How I'd wish to let go of myself in a fuller, deeper way than I ever did! An urge of surrendering falls upon me, hits me like a Sahara wind, blowing all residues of childhood away.

Yes, the gardens are vicious. Not only their abandon infects me, makes me want to kneel, lie, melt into the ground, liquefy. There are other ingredients—intricacy, secrecy, lacing. Vines hugging old stones. Violets hiding. Mushrooms peering out of the grass, smelling of fermentation. Roses crying petals onto the gravel. White. Red. Crimson. Pink. Myriads. Roses like rosaries. Pungency of invisible jasmine. Treacherousness of honeysuckle.

The buzz of a bee makes me jump aside, bump against him. He's just grabbed a butterfly, holding it between index and thumb. He laughs while he throws it under the collar of my blouse. I gasp, then I chase it downwards. The insect drunkenly staggers out, then it flies. I'm dizzy as well, and these are the grounds only. A preliminary, and they have lasted enough.

But we aren't alone. There are sisters, cousins. They are behind. The two of us proceed with the hastened beat of anticipation, this thing pushing us forward, separating us from the chaperoning cortege. Do we notice? We don't.

A brook leads to a pond. A willow's green, teary fingers brush the water. Can't do softer than that, or more thrilling. The pond quivers and shivers.

Let's go inside and have tea. The building looks solemn and cold. They all are, those turn-of-the-century villas. That's how they keep their secrets, lots, yet all of the same kind, exquisite and sinful. Illicit. Delightful. Cheap, truly, and that's why they are hidden. Predictable, and they get wrapped in mystery because of pure vanity. Still delightful.

Although marble, chill, gilded surfaces prevail, the house is full of recesses. I mean fabric, thick curtains and velvet bedspreads, tulle-screened canopies and pillows on couches, furry carpets and silken lightshades. That's what favors the sins to be committed. Fabric pads them and muddles them, softens them and conceals them. The house gathers them all.

I am ready. I have reached the right age. A bit green, but then it is tastier. When I sit in the living room for tea and scones I am molten lava. I am Niagara Falls. "Milk or lemon?" his mother inquires. She's assessing me.

I'm too short and too poor.

She won't go to her room before seeing I'm given a ride home. By the driver.

No farther did we read therein.

The villa is called Moonstone. A rock, straight from the moon, fell upon my chest. Why? It was a leisurely walk, an afternoon visit. Inno-cent. Introductory. What's the problem if teenage desire awoke right then, right there?

Whatever the problem was, it is durable. I will never be capable of removing the stone. It has crushed, crumbled something, scarred a star on my breast. Can't a star be beautiful? There are some you don't want to wear. This is ugly. I should call it an octopus, or a spider. A tarantula.

*

Years have past. I'm about to get another mark. Vertical, going down the length of my thigh. Going up, from the knee to where I have stopped it. Inner side.

We are in bed in another stoned-villa. This one belongs to my family, which makes it—how to put it—familiar? More familiar. I mean I can't be driven away. Beside the fact I have grown. Now I drive.

We have kept in touch. We have remained friends. We have sent postcards and phoned, sometimes met. Recently we have drawn nearer. We have taken long walks, sat on benches in front of the ocean at sunset, when it was getting chilly and we should have sought each other's arms. That we haven't. We have played it cool. He has only caressed my wrist, surrounded by a thin silver chain.

Is it gold? Is it my ankle? It is gold and it is my neck. Is he touching my neck? He must be. The Sahara wind blows in our face. Our eyes become teary. Here we can always count on wind, should we need it.

He's caressing my neck, embroidered by a thin golden chain. "Small things suit you," he says. They do. Suit me. Reach me. Choke me. Stick forever with me.

I don't answer. In spite of his touch nothing happens because, see, I have this scar on my chest (a tarantula niched between my breasts). There's a dam. His hand can't go further. *Dommage.*

We have boyfriends and girlfriends. Lovers, I mean other ones. We enjoy reporting about it. It is called spite, though it's kindly performed in our case. I tell him I've hooked up with a friend of his. He tells me he likes women with model bodies. I am one. But he's found another.

Still, we manage to end up in bed after a long lasting party, thanks to a shortage of rides (though the villas, over here, are contiguous to town. Though virtually you could walk anywhere. But the villas, remember, fall back in time. Extricating yourself becomes harder). We all camp in my family's dilapidated abode, sharing rooms, sheets, beds, bathrooms. Three of us occupy the main bedroom, solemn like a cathedral. The bed's huge, a plaza. A wide mirror faces it, a bit offset, enticing. A brass candelabra is atop. Obsolete toiletries—abalone, tortoiseshell, egret and peacock feathers, dead flowers—are all over.

Three of us collapse over the mattress. A girl is on my right, he on my left. We are joking and talking at various degrees of inebriation. Sleep is not on the menu. Some fun could be, or not.

We are past teenage. We have done things, even too many. We feel jaded. Sex is easy, whenever we like it. Opportunities are plenty, so they can be missed, in case. We have tried tricks. We could try some more, with no urgency. We have already partied in bed. We have watched and been watched. Tonight all is possible, or nothing, and it won't make a difference. So I think.

As exhaustion takes over, our talking finally ceases. On my right side, where the girl lies, there's stillness and silence. On my left side, the same thing. On my back, eyes wide open, I stare at the golden luster and I am peaceful.

At least so I think. Then his hand starts up from the cavity of my knee, slowly climbing the tenderness of my thigh. I didn't see it come. Didn't hear, didn't feel. I can't even discern his breathing, but I sense his calm.

And a zillion other things. Willow leaves over the surface of water. Shiver and quiver. Molten lava. Niagara Falls. None of it ever awoke during these years of exuberant, unleashed sex. Nothing will again. I am sure. I know it. It's already scarred in me, already choking me.

The girl on my right turns and tosses. She coughs. She's my best friend. Of course I should ignore her, but I don't think I can. Thinking is not the appropriate action to take, but I'm taking it. We should stop, pause at least. What does my girlfriend want? Should I ask? Should she participate? Should we share? Should the guy be in the middle?

Would she prefer watching? I am blocking his hand that has climbed all the way by now, like a pilgrim who walked on his knees to the sanctuary to win eternal pardon. Almost there, but I grab his wrist. So much larger than mine. So much stronger.

"Wait," I say—the best spell-breaker I know, the word that dispels all enchantments. "Wait, not now, not yet," the entire arsenal of counter-magic. We whisper a few quick replies. He does not want to share, I understand. Not at all. He's got a shirt on, grabbed a pillow, moved to another room. I'll see him in the morning.

Grandpa's gun was there, in the drawer, loaded with silver bullets, and I have killed the wolf. Grandma's pie was poisoned. I've killed lightheartedly, as the fairytale instructed me to do. I came back to

Mom's bed, well-behaved girl that I am. Well-behaved depraved girl.

Did I think killing wolves is good policy? Something you should do now and then, just to keep in shape? Why did I pull the trigger? Out of fear? Revenge?

Did I know wolves are an endangered species, about to go extinct?

Did I know I'd never find one again?

I would just be emblazoned with a scar on my thigh. A long strip of skin, clawed away. A torn piece of bark, showing a live texture of lymph. Ugly and obscene.

Deserved.

LIES THEY TELL

They tell lies about the body. When they say, for example, that it is one, the same, a continuum, holding all memories and emotions within. Indelibly emblazoned with every scar we got. False. Our body keeps changing. We shed skins as snakes do. It's a kind of miniature death, each time, with subsequent rebirth (if that makes sense). Our cells are replaced, in turns maybe, all sooner or later. Then the stuff we're made of is entirely new. We have become something else.

I can tell, because you were sitting before me and I didn't notice. I bent forward, having something to whisper in my colleague's ear. Careful not to disturb the play I spoke softly, very close to her neck. And to yours, since you sat beside her. I breathed just a millimeter away from your cheek, basking probably in your smell. Brushing your beard, your skin. But I didn't notice, which proves what I stated above.

I mean my body didn't react to your proximity. How is it possible? Because my mind didn't know? Come on! When did the mind have a say about attraction? Doesn't desire always fool it? Didn't we, I, fall in bed always mindlessly, or more often against my mind's warmest wishes? What made me react to you in the past didn't need awareness. It was merely instinctual, a matter of magnetism. Chemicals so powerfully stirred, they took action without me noticing. You know what I'm talking about.

Now, even if my brain had not added the parts, not done the multiplication—had I not labeled your presence with your identity—my body, if it were even partially what it previously was, should have performed its job. My hair should have stuck out (it's called horripilation), my glands should have poured sweat, I should have inexplicably blushed (vessels madly dilating, blood flowing towards the surface, eager to watch the show, enjoy the bullfight).

Isn't it how it goes? Reflexes occur. They take over, unless you employ self-control. That I could have. Having sensed, almost touched you, having been struck by an internal lightning, my heartbeat gone insane… Having finally recognized you, I could have checked myself from the heights of my wisdom, my seasoned matureness, and be-haved as if nothing had happened.

The point is, nothing did. That is only explainable if my body were changed. I don't mean modified. I mean substituted. Switched in its crib like a changeling.

Then I felt uncomfortable. Not emotional. Just annoyed by a purely rational concern. What if you had seen me? You might have thought I was I. Now don't get me wrong. I know it would have been natural. I haven't changed much externally. Something in my profile, highly rec-ognizable, would have rung a bell. You would have put a name on the picture and assumed (here comes the awkward part) that entity (name plus bodily appearance) corresponded to the person you once knew.

How embarrassing… both such misunderstanding and the impos-sibility, should the occasion arise, of explaining it. There is nothing to explain. What comes closest to reality is that I died too often. I could tell you that much but you wouldn't grasp it. Though you might have opinions about, even knowledge of death, that doesn't mean mine. Death is personal.

You would not, you couldn't possibly imagine… My accounts or de-scriptions would remain, as they say, a dead letter. Right! That must be where the expression takes roots. A "dead letter" is the attempt to give life to someone else's death.

I have died many times after we last met. Each resurgence was hard-er somehow, more hazardous. You can do it repeatedly (resurrecting yourself, like a phoenix) but it wears out eventually. The result is in-creasingly Zombiesque, Lazarus-like… I wish you'd see the bandages I can hardly conceal. Well, I wish you would not, or anyone else. They are my private affair.

I have died many times, then sewn back my carcass with care for resemblance. Not to fool anyone, just because of inertia, seeking some-thing familiar, a shape I was used to. Also, to avoid explanations. Do not think I wouldn't have liked to pick a new skin, sometimes, wipe off the past. Then I should justify myself, find excuses for those folks exclaiming, "you have changed, why did you?" That could break the dams. Searching for the most banal answer, I might let escape pieces of flesh, bloody rags, even severed limbs. The entire arsenal I thought I had disposed of.

That is why I kept it simple. I sew back a me as kin as possible to what people had in mind, with the left over parts, neither fit nor sufficient. When you die (not the last time but the previous ones—those preparatory mutations each of us endures, following random whims of what's called destiny, or luck) obviously something goes to waste. Pieces actually get ruined or burned out. Chunks of various amount and importance. It depends on the specific occurrence.

Some deaths of mine were routinary, consumption like, sneaky. Dull. Sordid but undramatic. Some were brutal, with loud explosions and consequent loss of bolts, nuts, rebuilding instructions. One of those impromptu catastrophes, dear, struck me recently. I am barely walking around, still experimenting with the taste of fresh air. With breathing, that in summary is all you need for resuscitating, as you learned in basic rescue training.

That is all you have to do—inhale, exhale then repeat ad libitum, ad nauseam, and your cells, after some erratic attempts, end approximately in the proper place. Your cells? New cells, recently fabricated. As we said some get lost, some perish. New ones pop up, insufficient. The original stock is never reconstituted. The promised refill is nothing but a dishonest ad, a marketing scam. New cells appear, resembling their deceased ancestors but knowing nothing. They have no memory, did not learn their history, none of it.

I am no more myself, believe me. Not my bodily self. I'm this shell broken and patched. A black and white shot of the original, fading in its turn. I so wish you wouldn't think I'm feigning indifference in your presence. I am in-different, alas, because I am different.

And what do I know? Maybe the same happened to you in the meanwhile. It happens to many (following the random caprice of what is called destiny, or luck). But the problem persists. Even if you died as frequently as I did, as I previously stated it's not the same death. We didn't die together. We diverged, we parted, we drifted away.

CHERRIES

It has been millennia since I last ate you. How did I dare, today, breaking the spell?

Your stem neatly detached by a twist of my fingers, your thick flesh with its sparkly aftertaste exploding on tongue, your pit so very small that for lack of practice I'm scared of swallowing it... I have missed a fruit in my mouth, especially a fruit like you.

Almost for a lifetime I've shied away, fearing a secret threat you concealed under gracious smoothness, under naïve alegria. Innocent, are you?

You came in brown bags, paper satchels. You came timely, on season, and we waited for you. Late May, early June. After the roses bloomed for the Virgin Mary, you wrapped up the sensuality of spring in a bloody sap precursor of luscious summer, of apricot, peach and plum prodigality.

You appeared, velvety, dense, a queen dressed up for a court dance, but your size made you childish. Cheerful ballerina, hand in hand with rosy-cheeked playmates twirling in brazen tutus. Caroling, playing hide and seek in a maze of dark leaves.

Ladder pushed against the trunk, basket hanging across a branch, neck bent backward I gazed up, my eyes lost in a crimson orgy. Happiness was too large for my shrinking heart. Cherries, I've left you behind, just where I left myself.

I don't know who kept going after the split. Who lived in my name. But it wasn't me.

THE THING I AM

B efore is a shadow.
   Before is a beret-basque inclined on the side, and plain features. Plain equals neutral. An upper lip where hair is expected to appear, and then thicken.

Expected by whom? By the shadow, lingering for a while before vanishing. Not entirely, though.

We have asked about breasts getting rounded and larger. It will happen over time, we were answered. We have waited a day or two, then we have gaged the thickness above and below the nipple. It felt slightly increased, no doubt. Happily, we have reported the news and someone has laughed. We have not been offended.

We have visited the large bedroom mirror and been surprised. Our hair was getting longer. Things were changing, not sure in which direction. Hair was black and curled. Pulling the curl we discovered a remarkable stretch. Things were progressing, expanding no matter how.

But there is before. Short hair, a round face, nondescript. Sitting in a bed surrounded by bars like a cage. A cage can be lovely. It prevents you from falling out. That's a body's natural tendency—rolling out of beds, magnetized by those small carpets appositely laid on the floor. Carpets are soft, thank god, yet not enough.

In the cage another round-headed thing has been delivered. The thing bobs. The head bobs... well, the entire thing bobs. It's a little brother, whatever it means. An intrusion. An addition? A subtraction, perhaps?

We are waiting for stains on underwear. They do not appear. We are imagining it, then we are hallucinating it. We are imagining infinitesimal spills of brown rust. Then we are hallucinating a pink dot, the side of a quarter. We agonize for the vision to materialize as if waiting for a miracle. Miracles are out of control. Agony is consuming.

There's before and it becomes remote. We are soaked in the bathtub with some little brother. Little brothers have multiplied. Brothers have things that Mother calls peas, birds, fishes. They look neither vegetal nor animal, unless… maybe fat slugs. Unobtrusive, cute, certainly not worrisome. They get vigorously washed like the rest of brothers' bodies, and our own.

We have a cut under the belly. Red inside, more intensely then anywhere else in the body. Occasionally, the cut hurts (that is kind of logical) but not always, and it is pretty much out of the way, so we don't really care about it. Still, the useful data is brothers don't have it.

This is the main point. A clear definition. We are not brothers. We are sister. We haven't yet appraised it as an advantage or disadvantage. Probably, an advantage. It would be preferable. We'll go with advantage.

Until when, after a good sparring, we prevail and put our knee on the chest or back of a defeated brother (who in the meantime irresistibly giggles and tries to escape, to prevail in his turn). But we cannot bang our fists on our chest, orangutan style. It is sudden. Knuckles bump against acorn-like formations that weren't there yesterday. They are painful. This is very strange, most unfair, sadly handicapping. This is maiming our bravery, heroism, righteous pride.

Then embarrassment comes. Brothers taken away from her room. A room for her alone. Her room. She has a room for her, alone. One bed. Very small. A very small room. She cannot watch football on TV with her brothers. She is sent away.

Then comes more embarrassment. Father slaps her when she wears the things Grandma knitted for her with such love… sweaters, dresses, hoses. Father slaps her because those clothes no more suit her. She cannot figure why. She is afraid each time that she gets dressed. No, she doesn't like to be slapped, or embarrassed, or scared. She is definitely she.

She has a boyfriend, the first one she will make love to. There were previous boys, previous love, without any making. She has imagined making it. She has hallucinated it. Suddenly, it has become urgent. This time is the one.

Now the boyfriend… he has a beard, black, thick, dense, impenetrable. Now the boyfriend is going to declare himself. Declare? She already knows what she needs to. He is about to confess his feelings. Intentions. There's some ritual talking he has to spit out, but that happens slowly.

As slowly as you can bear. It happens on a very long road bordered by rows of tall trees. It's a large road as well, paved, but on both sides there's a slope, muddy, kind of dangerous.

The two of them are walking, not sure where directed. He is talking, and his talking is getting to the point very slowly. While he talks, he unconsciously and irrepressibly veers to the left. She is left of him. He bends left, pushing her closer and closer to the slope. She tries to redirect him with no pushing, no telling. Gently, she tries to redress, straighten up, to proceed in parallel. Straight and parallel, the road neatly shared by two moving bodies. Two. Moving. Bodies. There's no way. She feels anguished. She's afraid she'd fall down the slope. Anguish is consuming.

He has declared himself and that's all for now. Consequences are for later. Oh well. But he's given her a token, a talisman. Not a ring, no. A rabbit paw. A dead rabbit paw. Elongated. Soft. Furry. Once an animal thing, but now what? She is holding the paw when he sees her to the bus. He is sending her home with their pact defined and consequences to come.

Their pact sealed by the rabbit paw she is holding, while she waves goodbye.

She is afraid and slightly disgusted. She would like to drop the paw but she knows she can't. She has to hold it, this thing once alive, this amalgam of fat, hair, flesh, bone. Blood stained? Not any more. Not yet.

EDUCATION

Grandma taught me how to be a proper lady. She tried. Her instructions came nicely and I didn't look at them closely. She loved me. I loved her. I couldn't imagine displeasing her. I obeyed her and it wasn't hard.

She taught me how to become a lady (she tried) though I was half of one. Dad's side wasn't genteel. She ignored it. Still, she said I resembled Dad like a drop of water. Strange expression... there aren't two drops of water alike.

Grandma instructed me through examples of her past in which I saw my future. I grew up with detailed knowledge of the roaring twenties and erroneous expectations. Retro, romantic tastes... wicker furniture, beaded lampshades, silk pillows. Hiding a handkerchief in my sleeve rather than using Kleenexes.

When I would grow up I'd folk dance, Grandma said. Great fun, appropriate and innocent. I looked forward to it more than I thought of schools or careers. I looked forward to knitting and marmalades. Also poetry, in spare inspired moments. On a balcony, watching the clouds.

I expected a life made of cameos, full of domestic chores plus chaste entertainment. And I'd glide through it unscathed, perhaps with a zest of melancholy as suited to the early twentieth century, a time squeezed, crushed between two wars.

None of it would happen, of course. My apprenticeship was entirely wasted, but who cared? Grandma loved me. She did.

CAMEO

1

Off-white, peers from behind the piano, stands against the dark wooden floor, indecipherable in the dim light. Probably a slip of paper, a note, the corner of an envelope. I will pick it up as soon as...

A slice, moonish, shell-like. Hardboiled egg peel? Untidy. Did I drag my food to the living room? A shard of tortilla bread.

It's a photograph. An old polaroid, colors gone. Mother... a silhouette surrounded by rings of yellow, rust, brown, like haloes of dampness. Truly, remnants of photo pigments. The figure looks abandoned, lost. Delicately, I lift the small scrap between index and thumb.

It was cut with a pair of children scissors so blunt, they have left around the edges a thin folded rim. And the shape is irregular. Elongated circle, thick oval, you name it. Has someone wished to fit it inside a frame? Have I? Perhaps long ago. Maybe a locket? Did I possess one? Should I get one and wear it?

Not a small box around my neck, please. Small prison. Small coffin.

I would rather drop Mom into my purse, holding the pic by its emptiest spot, an edge from which impressions have vanished. This positions the figurine (head and half a torso) upside down. Reversed like in utero, about to be born.

Funnel. Calyx. Bellflower. Inland sea. Lagoon and sublime explorers, within, look for a way out.

2

As I worked on a movie set in a remote region, arid shore squeezed between mountains and ocean, I was accidentally trapped inside a small chapel.

I had prepared it for the next day shooting, a funeral. Dusted. Swept. Disposed containers for large floral arrangements, neatly dressed the altar with lace, rolled a crimson rug through the nave, all the way to the door… the last touch, last chore of my day, as in spite of the unvaried, thick penumbra of the place, I could tell it was late. Then I realized the door had been locked.

No other opening besides two narrow slits in the apse, very high, out of reach. Two thin gothic windows, blocked by panes of stained glass. Did they open and close? Were they sealed? Useless questions, as the answers wouldn't make any difference.

I climbed on frigid stone to one of the windows, unhinged the glass pane, dropped it down the wall without a concern. I contortioned myself like a reptile, like a circus artist or a consummate burglar, squeezing through the gap. I jumped. As I landed on dirt I ran as if followed by demons, yet inhabited by an exhilarated feeling of lightness.

3

Sit at the very end of the table. Get up frequently and suddenly, wander to the kitchen with an excuse, go find where the restrooms are. Front door? Make sure you can reach it rapidly. Exit sign? Park on street. Avoid basements. Sit on top of the retaining wall, your legs dangling, tasting the other side. Locate the big hole in the fence. Toss the pillow, far. Undo blankets and sheets at the bottom of the bed, let your feet air. If the seat near the aisle is taken, get the window. Look up, at the sky.

Escape chapel. Escape coffin. Escape funeral. Escape death. Escape uterus, dive into the bloody channel headfirst. Escape locket, escape photograph. Ink fades out and the background becomes sheer, translucent. Oval shard of paper a broken eggshell. Nest disintegrated, small twigs pulverized on grass. Mother smaller and smaller, crawling backwards, the past a faint bell, a tocsin.

Run as if you were followed by demons. Run as if you had wings.

HER KIND

Equal. Mute. Contained. A tunnel.

Life is a tunnel. Two holes at the two extremities. They call them morning, night.

Two holes. You get out of the first one. You crawl down a ladder. The rungs are kind of shaky, set far apart. You are afraid you'd slip in between. You could. You have lost enough weight.

You could even squeeze behind the drywall, in the tiny space left between it and the concrete. You have been thinking about it. Did you? When your son's stuffed animal fell. You have spent hours fishing for the toy. Why? Did you have that much time to waste? Were you seeking some perverse satisfaction? You have rescued the toy with a hooked rod, after having relentlessly probed depth and darkness. It was not needed. You know it, do you?

Life is a tunnel, and that is reassuring. You only have to squeeze out of a hole, then crawl to the next hole that will bring you back to the first hole, although it isn't the same, properly speaking. It is still number one, just another number one. I mean, there is this countless series of ones and twos, like in square dance. Exactly. You are familiar with the concept, quite a simple one. Square dancing. A long row of couples. Very, very long, a bunch of people, all different so to speak. Diverse, so to speak. And the couples are numbered as follows: one, two, one, two, one, two. Either you are a one or a two. Then, at some point, the ones become twos and vice versa.

Does it happen with night and day? It could. Meaning, there's increasing smoothness in their alternating. Homologation. If you crawl lowly, evenly, head down, perfectly mute, in the end night and day truly resemble each other. I promise.

Now don't look around. Look at the task. Focus on your task. Stay with it. When you are almost finished think about the next one, without leaving a gap. Careful. I know that you're found of interstices. You like squeezing in. Crawling, coiling, hiding.

In your bed, for instance. Bed is an interstice. You like squeezing in it, do you? And dream. Tell me, though. What can you possibly dream of?

*

There is a pole. Old style. A telegraph pole. Do you remember those? Not a phone tower, no. A brown telegraph pole, made of wood. Those have personality. All around, the landscape is desolate. I don't mind. Who cares about the landscape? The sky is afire... sunset must be close, but I'm not sure of time and it doesn't matter. It does not because I am tied, here, my foot shackled to the pole, though the chain is quite long. Very long, in fact. When you're chained, time doesn't matter at all. You can't switch to the next activity. You can't progress.

My activity is repetitive but intense. I run forward, to the end of the line. End of the chain, I mean. When the chain stops me I turn around. I come rest my back against the wooden pole, which is just wide enough. A nice break of varied duration—as I was saying, time doesn't count. When I'm rested, I start over.

Forward, obviously, is everywhere. All is ahead of me, but the pole. The loop drawn by the chain around the wood is quite loose, easily slips around. I run at three hundred and sixty degrees, with complete freedom of perspective. I have traced all possible radiuses to this circumference. Then I have started again, randomly. Believe me, there's no end to this task.

There is joy in my doing. My body exults in the effort. Speed exhilarates me and I'm growing faster and faster. I've the feeling my muscles get stronger by the hour. The minute? I have no clue. Again, time has no relevance. But speed does, and I'm going faster and faster. You see, I thrust myself forward without any restraint. It is dazzling, extreme. I can do it only because I'm fastened... You should try, there's no risk whatsoever, no fear. At the end of the run, when I'm about to stop dead, yanked back, I slightly levitate from the ground. I swear... it started happening at a certain point, just a minimal lift. Now it never fails to occur. At the end, with the last step or two, I am suspended for a fraction of breath, a mere inhalation. This is what I look for, three hundred and sixty degrees around. This is what I live for.

*

90

Wake up. You have been turning and tossing in your bed. You have been moaning. You are drenched in sweat. I'm afraid you got a bug. Take your temperature. You should stay in bed today. Call work, say you are sick. Why don't you? Why don't you ever take a break? See you tonight.

*

Life has narrowed down to a tunnel made of plain, equal segments. I like the routine, the predictability. This is all I can handle, a segment, a piece of tube. I don't mind the material. Plastic would do. Could be one of my child's toys. A toy would be fine.

I don't need diversions. They unnerve me. They hinder my progress. They make me vacillate. I like snug and narrow. More than all, I like linear.

I don't eat more than necessary. It is a distraction. Less and less is necessary. I know, it is a vicious circle. Habit, someone would say. The less I eat, the less I require and that helps the linearity that is paramount, as you have guessed, leading me through the tunnel.

Equal segments. Contained. Mute.

Now you ask if there is an end to the tunnel. Why should there be? What should I expect at the end? A wide expanse? Freedom?

You mean borderless chaos. You mean the sky. But I wasn't made for the sky.

The less you eat, the more your bones become brittle and the more they break. Small bones, those with the width of twigs like fingers, toes, ribs, break quite easily. Ribs can spontaneously break with a cough, a laugh, a brisk motion. I don't laugh. Sometimes I move briskly. Recently I'm coughing a lot. I break plenty of ribs. They hurt moderately and then heal, spontaneously. I'm not in control of my ribs.

There's a sense of exhilaration when they break. For a minute (is it so?) I am confused. I don't know what happened. There's a snap, and a sense of humiliation. Then I enjoy it. The suspension. The looseness. The small gap, that hint of a way out.

My ribcage has broken all over, only, not at the same time. It has broken, I could say, at three hundred and sixty degrees. As long as I'm so thin, so ethereal it will keep breaking. Could I breathe more easily through this loosened cage? Will it end up bursting, exploding? I dream about it, in those segments I call nights.

But you see, I am not a bird, wasn't made that. Will not become one, not in this life.

In this life, I crawl. And I dream.

CONCENTRIC CIRCLES

During the first three months she appeared in my dreams. She was old and a child at the same time, always wanting to play. I organized balls, picnics, games, all possible festive event, maybe to compensate for a loss, giving her a crash course on something she had missed. Catching up with a part of life Grandma hadn't truly perused, music, dance, colors, shine.

I was giving the parties her dad should have thrown in his turn-of-the-century mansion, with all of his freaking money. But he sent her to a boarding house and forgot about her, did he? Her mom had died of childbirth. Her stepmom…

In our gatherings Grandma amused herself with great gusto. She wore fancy clothes, tender hues laced with silver and gold. She said little but couldn't stop laughing. Neither could I.

The dream cycle culminated with a scene I'll never forget. One more party, on the grand side. She showed up in flapper attire, nineteen twenties fashion. Many layers of pink, purple, crimson. And we danced and we danced, but a zest of sadness lingered. While we twirled she said she had something to ask.

I should push her away, she said. Time for her to reach another circle, a more distant ring, more removed crown of reality. She had to further dissolve and she would. But she didn't want to. Could I?

What, Grandma?

I pushed her while dancing. Little pulses at first, then gradually stronger. It was hard. She was light, but heavy at the same time. And there was that gloom, typical of the moments when you have to make choices and they split you. They tear you apart.

I woke up in a sweat. She didn't come back.

VERTIGO

I am six years old on the 28th of December, nineteen-o-eight. Six or seven? I will never know. All municipal archives will be lost in the earthquake. Are being. Were.

I have sat on a pillar all day. Someone put me there and told me to stay. Who was it? Mother has died last year. I will never see her again, not even in pictures. Her grave will be swallowed by the seism. Was. And the archives, I said, are all gone by now. No trace will remain of Mother besides what I keep in mind. A small, square sepia snapshot.

I am in my nightgown. They have snatched me from bed in the dark. Run, run, run, that's all I understood and then it was dawn. I have sat on this pillar all day. Where is it? Not sure. The world looks like an egg fallen from the nest. Have you seen one? Shards all over, a shattered china cup. And a sad, translucent, gluey mess. Even if you did nothing, you feel bad when you see a broken egg.

This morning I don't. My head is full of cotton. I am cold, my brain must be frozen. I am in my nightgown, long and thick, still I am shivering. It's winter. The sky looks like milk.

I see chaos and dust. I hear screaming. I am not hungry, no.

The only picture of me you ever saw was taken years later. I had forgotten it all.

My braid, black, reaches my knees. Fashion favors long hair. I am wearing an unadorned grey robe, my face a plain oval, heavy featured and sheepish. My eyes black, like my hair. In the photo I am profile, a book in my hand. Looking down at the page, but straight like a trunk. Like a column, a vertical drop perpendicular to the ground. No. No twist and no twirl, no curvaceous grace.

"Beautiful," I confessed while I rocked you over my knee, "I never was." I couldn't help giggling, discreetly as I did everything. But I laughed each time I repeated the mantra to you. "Beautiful," I intoned, irrepressibly chuckling, "I..."

I couldn't go on. "Never..." "Was," you said with a smile.

Please remember me.

*

Could you also be me?

Borrow, absurd as it sounds, my blond hair, so light they thought me albino. Thin like flax, straight like rain. The curls would come later. Let us disregard curls, lipstick, stilettos, pencil skirts, padded blouses, all the fifties glamour. Let us hold onto the beginning of June, nineteen-forty. I am flax-haired, slanted eyes of pale steel, pretty face. Little queen, where did I come from?

A large bow in my hair, I am brought home from school in our shiny Traction Avant. At a brisk stop the door slams open. I fall. Unscathed, yet completely terrified, I scramble back on my feet.

Later I'm in the kitchen, still shaking, but a spread of small cauliflowers distracts me. They are in the sink, with the water in which someone just boiled them. Cute, small canary blooms float on surface. Unreflectively, I thrust my hand in to pick one of them, maybe only caress it. My mouth opens but I can't scream.

A bright yellow star looms through the blister that was my palm.

No one pays heed to these misadventures of mine. War just started. Dad will be called within days. German, British, American soldiers will occupy town for the next five years, while I'll slowly elongate, blossom, ripe, my hair darkening, curling. But I know you don't care about what comes after. I know you want me blue, sailor dressed, striped collared. White socks, black Mary Janes, polite, naïve, scared. You have seen me this way, do you?

Take me, then.

*

I have taken you both.

I have put you in a same cardboard box, not even too large. One accommodates all. Three of us. Girl. Girl. Girl. Brown, blond, brown. Pretty or plain. Afraid, still upright. We fit into this package I am leaving right here, in the closet. Orderly, dusted off, without label.

I have been you as you asked.

I am not saying.

It's no more I recalling.
I have ceased remembering.
She is coming.

YOUNG PENELOPE

She liked carrying her supper outdoors, she said, very far from the house, past gardens and orchards. Sneaking through the kitchen door, her palm held over the bowl like a lid, a spoon loose inside her apron pocket, drumming against her thigh, she gradually yet decisively hastened her pace. For no reason, fleeing nothing, only moved by necessity. And a sort of exhilaration, perhaps.

As she reached the usual spot she sat on a concrete step, lowering herself slowly, slowly, her back to a chunk of wall against which she could have leaned but didn't. The place was a forsaken construction site, an aborted something. Maybe a stable or a barn, forever unfinished. One of those things the master's eye obliterates until they become invisible.

The ugly thing, the rubble of bricks and leftover boards felt cozy. It provided a kerchief of shade, the small drop she needed, without being an obstruction to the rest.

The rest was what she sought. Immensity, though she couldn't have named it.

The only way she was able to define it, half a century later, was "a kind of light... blinding... not quite..." Then her voice split, frayed, pulverized itself.

The interviewer neither had much imagination, nor had researched ahead if not superficially. Otherwise she would have immediately pictured what the aging queen tried to recall.

She (the interviewer, distracted as she looked intent, face down, thumb lingering on the recording button of her phone) would have known the borderless expanse of the plains, the blurring of green into gold, the unforgiveness of ocher and rust, the ebullient red. How the sky started loosening, its seams coming undone, imperceptibly sinking at its center, an immense parachute lowering itself, mesmerized by the ground. How the brush of earth and sky caused sparkles, a dizzying shimmer, a temblor.

So this is what she seeks, each time. Gravity.

She isn't hungry yet. She places the bowl at her side. On the step there's just enough room. She needs for the light, the air, the endless view, the stillness, subtle smells, dulled noise, subdued presence, remoteness, to fill all of her cells before she can fill her stomach.

That she does later, apparently sluggishly but with sheer de-light, spoonful at a time.

The rough pudding (yesterday's bread dipped in milk, sometimes a sprinkle of cinnamon, sometimes lemon zest) sits on her tongue while she stares at nothing, soaked within the landscape. Then all is tranquility.

This is what she was seeking.

Eternity. She likes how everything curves, the horizon, the entire view converging into a single point of perspective, tiny dot, herself. Her body is V-shaped like a funnel, sucked in by her iliac bones fused to the concrete supporting her weight. And the bowl, loaded with food, slowly bares its bottom against which the spoon, oval, deep, rests like a vessel buried underwater, peacefully sleeping in sand.

Everything bends gently, irreversibly. All is sickle. All is moon, though the light just before sunset is blinding.

On her way back, she hooks her finger through the handle of the empty bowl. She always picks the same one, once provided with two symmetrical twirls coiling on both sides. Then a twirl fell off.

She always picks the same lopsided container. The spoons vary, as she grabs them in haste from the kitchen drawer, where spares are relegated when the set they belonged to have fallen out of grace. Incomplete, too many broken or lost, obsolete.

So the spoons are always different, and gorgeous. Gilded or silver coated, nicely moired by oxidation, curlicued, ornate, emblazoned with the royal escutcheon. She sees them without seeing, though. Her eyes...

When she retraces her steps, her bowl dangles by her finger. It drums rhythmically on the side of her thigh, which bring several marks. Faint bruises, veering from pink to dark as the sky does, right now.

GIRL BY THE WINDOW

Doctors meet at regular intervals to discuss the patients. Eli, the chief nurse, attends those reunions. A few medical students are welcome to sit, listen, take notes.

I have followed the chief nurse to the meeting room, pen and pad bulging in the front pocket of my blouse. She stops on her way to fasten a helmet strap. For some reason, those supposed to keep headwear at all times still manage to unbutton it (we are at the Children Hospital, Neuropsychiatric Ward). Fascinated by her brisk, expert fingers, I wait until she finishes. Her mouth squeezes in concentration. She is square-faced, lipless and gently whiskered. Down to earth and authoritative, incredibly efficient. I always try to enter the meeting room right behind her, shielded by her reassuring presence.

We sit on metal chairs by the door. As I wait I open my pad, pen in hand. Eli doesn't need writing tools. Luminaries in white coats perch on leather armchairs. A long table, in front of them, bears a bunch of light colored folders. One of the doctors gingerly picks a file, quickly gazes at the front page. Wearily, he throws his glasses upon the typed words, fingers lifted to his nose bridge as if squeezing out a significant thought. Perhaps hold it.

Last name, first name. Diagnoses are usually skipped. The cases here discussed are inpatients and we know them quite well. Once in, they are not quickly dismissed, rarely transferred. Medications are listed, followed by cryptic comments, incidental discussions about a particular brand, dosage, synergy, side effect. A correction is inked down, then highlighted. Elizabeth will take care of it.

Next! Down the pile we go smoothly, unless something new was reported about a specific patient. Perhaps counseling, psycho or occupational therapy have started. Any improvement so far? Or a crisis took place. Rare instances. Usually these sessions are boring as hell and, for this particular ward, on the depressive side.

As if she knew it, Maria Soccorro Del Sol wanders in when her file is up. Yet, when a dull monotone utters: "Del Sol, Maria," then hesitates, then… "Soccorro" (they always seem to forget the second half of her name) she doesn't blink. I can't recall if she is deaf. Very likely. She stares at a large window opposite to the door, where she is clearly directed. And you can sense nothing will stop her.

No, not by the look on her face. That doesn't reveal a thing. Her eyes are misaligned, crossed with strabismus and consequently unfocused. Her features are motionless, limp like a rubber mask. She is so pale she looks like a walking moon, her skin waxen, her hands two bleak bundles abandoned on her thighs. Slowly, she drags her feet an inch at a time. Yet you can feel a current, a magnet, a steel wire pulling her somnambulic self towards her goal.

A soft curtain made of powdery layers of gauze, one peach, one periwinkle, another pea green, screens the windowpanes. I have noticed it before, by and large the prettiest sight in the room. Soccorro might have spotted it from the corridor. Perhaps she remembered it. Maybe she came on purpose to meet with those rainbow veils.

Now she stands by the wall and—perfectly still, a sphinx, hieratic, intent—she studies the sides of the curtain, as if evaluating how accurately the hem has been sewn while pondering her future course of action. Pull? Tear down? Crumple? Bite? Perhaps munch or kiss.

Meanwhile, her case has been reviewed and my memory refreshed. Soccorro is one of the oldest inpatients, ripe for transfer to an adult facility. You sure wouldn't tell. Her body is a twig, fragile, tiny, breakable. For appearance sake (nothing notable has been said) I jot a few lines on my pad. When I look up, she has vanished.

Not exactly. Wiggling on my chair I see her lying horizontally across the windowsill, which luckily is two feet high from the floor. She almost fits, bunched up, her knees bent towards her chest. She has partially wrapped herself with the bottom edge of the curtain. A fringe brushes her face.

Her small figure is embedded in the drapery, odalisque like, as if she were modeling for a painter or if she were a diva, about ready to exhale her dramatic solo. Of course, none of it applies to her looks, genderless, ageless, unexpressive, remote. Rather than using props in order to strike a pose, she has smoothed herself into the landscape, quietly objectifying her presence, swallowed by the décor.

No one has reacted to her entrance, as it was expected I guess. She doesn't hear or talk, doesn't communicate. She is far out, severed from our shared reality, husked inside her own world. Patients like her are allowed to freely circulate in absence of dangerous behaviors.

She has crossed the room on tiptoe, almost gliding, levitating on an invisible cushion of air, detached from the ground, with no sign of noticing surrounding humans. Likewise, no surrounding human has betrayed noticing her. No one presently glances at her reclined silhouette. At this fallen caryatide, this wrecked Neptune's angel.

My eyes stare at my scribbles but my mind is off. My thoughts wander to the grocery store where I will buy dinner. The afternoon's winding down and I am getting tired, distracted, sweet impatience tickling my limbs. How long will this... As I come back to the present moment I perceive something, a shift in the air, a slight turbulence that makes my eyes lift, seek the curtain.

Without much change in posture and certainly none on her face, Soccorro has crumpled up her hospital gown—rough linen printed with minute hierogliphs—and she is touching herself. Calmly masturbating, as if knitting away in front of a television set. She is discreet, unobtrusive, and yet the unmistakable rhythm of her hand disturbs the air particles. It calls for attention. Just mine? No one else looks in her direction.

On the table, two folders are left. The meeting reaches its end. We all wish to be finished.

So does Soccorro. She has extracted a stuffed animal from her gown's capacious front pocket. A quite battered toy and yet soft, I am sure, candy-colored. She is stroking her genitalia with it, faster and faster. The toy, bright, large, ostensible, adds a touch of grotesque to the scene, now hard to be ignored. A hint of provocation? Only in the observer's eye. Soccorro doesn't mean it. She is alone at the moment. She is always alone, at least not with us.

Leaning on her side like a dining Roman empress, the girl reaches orgasm when the last folder is closed. The pile pushed towards the center of the table, white-clad bodies concertedly rise. They greet noisily, and heavily walk away.

I stay seated. Her pleasure was noticeable. Her features came alive for a second, a fit, a release, then the closest to a smile I ever saw on her exiguous face, as a drip of saliva graced the corners of her lips. The hand holding the toy went suddenly limp, yet didn't let go. The other hand clawed at the curtain instead, squeezing it like a sponge.

Elizabeth, straightening armchairs au passage, pushing them squarely around the table, marches up to the window. She takes Socorro's hand. She helps her to stand up. Hand in hand they walk out, or else Eli does, carrying the girl along as if she were collecting a lost pen, an abandoned blouse. Yet considerately, kindly. Soon the room will be locked. The girl follows the nurse, easy, easy, barely brushing the floor, stuffed animal hanging by the tip of her lifeless fingers. Knocking at her calf like a pendulum bob, a bell clapper.

LESSON

Once, for a change, he is joyful. Almost happy. Standing at the door of his bedroom, the sanctuary where he always retires after lunch, he holds a book. His finger rests inside, marking the page.

Father reads an average of two titles a week. It's a habit that he made in his youth, trying to catch up with ignorance and build his homespun culture. Father is a natural born intellectual, sprung forth from complete illiteracy.

Early afternoon. As usual, he will begin his siesta with a title he likes, to ease relaxation. But, unheard of, he wants to read a quote out loud. To me? I happen to be the audience he needs. He talks slowly, padding each word with a very slight coat of silence. Like a golden halo, a suspension, maybe because the phrase is in English, a language Dad doesn't speak. Neither do I. Still, *"Everything of beauty is a joy forever,"* he spells and by miracle, by a sort of transubstanciation, I understand.

My eyes are riveted upon his shy, strange, precious smile, the thing I will remember, the greatest prodigy of all.

LAMENT

Sitting on a brand new bench, painted green like a flag, she cries. Painted green like a Christmas tree, like an emerald. She cries, her thin, flattened hair flushed down her sallow cheeks, small nose, narrow forehead, drowning her in sorrow.

Her collapse makes me vulnerable. Also mute. A witness. I don't hug her. I don't even touch her, sensing I shouldn't intrude. Her pain doesn't need sharing. Compassion is a strange invention. Her pain is fierce and wild, untamed like her falling hair.

She misses him. She misses him.

I tip on the edge of the bench. I lean forward for my elbows to reach the fence surrounding the pond, right in front of us. A small lake, deep, somber and smooth. In its center, an islet planted with tall, bushy trees. Mysterious.

I remember rowing a boat over there, years ago. With her? Him? The three of us? Finding eggs of aquatic birds in the underwood. Gathering blue feathers. Turquoise blue. Saying we would keep them forever. Rowing back in the afternoon sun.

Which bird's…

She keeps sobbing. I feel her body at my side, near and distant, while I stare at the water. My eyes hurt of being too open, too wide. They are full of nothing else but cool colors, shimmering shades. They scan the shifting surface as if they could pierce it, see through.

Then I see the birds at the bottom. Turquoise blue, like the feathers I recalled a minute ago. Like peacocks but smaller, the size of coy fish. They aren't fish, though. They are birds, blue, like jewels.

Underwater. They must be a reflection, of course. Look up. They must be flying by. Don't miss them. Three large birds, aqua-colored, mirrored by muddy waters. Don't miss them.

There are only three things—life, death, memory. Struck by a wave of impromptu weakness I would like to weep, but I can't. She is still at it, and pain cannot be synchronous in spite of common beliefs. It needs to be expressed in turns, with alternate motions, side to side, up and down, see-saw, swing, like walking, like flapping wings. I am the dry end for now, the extremity of the oar firmly anchored into the oarsman's hand.

Therefore, I am at the mercy of thoughts I cannot dilute in tears. They keep hammering my mind, spat out by a robotic typing machine, unbeknownst to myself, my thoughts.

There are only three things. Only two, life and memory.

Life is this, the humid, phlegmatic noise of sobs tapering down. The faint smell of unwashed hair. In a minute, I shall turn and meet her swollen eyes, find something to say, stand up, grab my purse. Then we'll probably walk. Go somewhere, which is definitely life — a sense of direction if vague, pointless. But still.

Memory! I was forgetting about it. Thick and rich, multilayered, yet it tends to be obliterated as soon as life shows its face. It is one or the other. They hardly coexist. They alternate. They need to take turns. One leg, then the other. One arm. Swim. Up and down. Flap your wings.

There are only two things, say my thoughts.

Where did the birds go? I have omitted to look up and now it is too late. My eyes are feeling sore, anyway. The sky might be too bright. I don't dare looking up, as I don't dare turning her way. Neither will I bend forward again, to find solace, distraction, in the scrutiny of shallow waters. I already know the birds — their reflections — have gone. These things are fugacious. These epiphanies. Beauty.

So I rest my gaze on a frontal level, neutral, casual, nonchalant. And I see the islet, of course, shifted to the side as if for courtesy, to give right of passage.

We were young when we found the eggs and feathers. I don't know if we were happy. I don't think so, but I cannot tell because memory doesn't keep feelings. It comes clean, in polished fragments, edges neatly dusted off. The glue of feelings, in spite of common beliefs, has gone brittle and crumbled away.

Earlier, as she started moaning, she has murmured things that didn't need answers. She has muttered the usual, how she misses him, cannot live without him. I have said nothing at all. She has stopped talking. Now she is done crying, at last.

Her breakdown has made me brittle, undone. I have felt my seams surreptitiously loosening, threads pulled out by a mischievous hand. I also miss him. I do. But his absence is so very wide, I can't focus.

And I cannot cry if someone else presently does it. We must take turns. There is limited room, life affirms, for extreme emotions. Momentarily I shall suspend mine.

There is only one thing. Memory.

OPEN WOUNDS

Lily died at two and a half. She was his first daughter.

Uncle had married quite late. When I was a child he was single, and he used to tell me that he would become a pope. Of course I believed him.

Then he abruptly introduced me to his secret fiancée. Beatrix had auburn pigtails like Pippi Longstocking. She taught English, for us an exotic language, and she wasn't born in the island we came from. She was from the main land, from the opposite shore (Uncle told me she had cast a spell across waters, looking out of her window, I believed him). I liked her on the spot. Forget about papacy. She did things Mother didn't, like swimming, sunbathing, playing ball on the beach and bike riding.

Beatrix marked a step into modernity, a bridge through generations, freshening our slightly stale family flavor. Uncle rejuvenated by marrying her, even more with the birth of their daughters.

They had five girls and Lily was first. She fell ill during her third summer, desperately seeking sugar and water. She had diabetes in a little known, lethal form, but they didn't lose hope. It all lasted less than six months. In an expensive clinic, abroad, the child suddenly died.

With my parents, I met Uncle and Aunt at the airport to give them a ride home. Beatrix cried very quietly. Uncle turned towards me, pulling something out of his pocket. A doll. Pretty, pretty, pretty little nurse, red cross on her apron.

Lily sent it to you, he said. He wasn't crying. But how softly he spoke. He barely whispered. And that crack in his voice, as if each word scorched his mouth.

Lily sent it, he said. I believed him.

NIGHT VISION

Once again, the woman who had lost her son shared her story.
I had heard it before. And she wasn't the only woman-who-had-lost-her-son I had heard talk. I remembered them all. All the women, the stories, words carving my chest, words of panic and un-healable pain.

Un-healable. Such a paradox in the world where I live, where these women lived or live. A world where we hear of trouble and we instantly seek cures, solutions, where the idea of "incurable" seems weirdly obsolete.

Stigma. What is it? We don't wear it anymore.

Then the woman who in the blink of an eye had lost her only son, loving, happy, young, talented, shared her tragedy, her irreparable loss and we, the small group of women there gathered for the most trivial reasons, stood up.

One by one we hugged her and she let us do it, and she embraced back with great strength, but softly. She embraced back with wholeness. And that wholeness, I felt, was like a plant.

Her thin body was like a twig, like those reeds that thrive by the water's edge, inconspicuous but flexible, wiry, resistant. That, I couldn't understand. The resistance.

Of course she had a name, but I called her June in my mind.

Though each time that it was repeated her story grew richer in details, as if slowly, slowly, June found the courage of peeling a bandage off a huge open wound, I did not know when her son had passed. Why did I call her June?

She looked young and strong, like a sapling. Now and then she looked like a knot, a bundle, like a crimson spoonful of raw… pain isn't the right word. Grief isn't either. Both are too dull in color. Her shade was more screaming, more desperate.

And yet she was composed, dignified, didn't try to elicit compassion, didn't indulge. No. The story of the dead son simply occurred. It materialized itself, rolling out of her mouth like a stream of rust, scarlet, pink, effervescent, bursting, cascading bubbles. Sunbeam, laser beam, thunderbolt, tide of electricity cutting the room in half, running out to the street, seeking escape, unstoppable.

She was not the only woman who had lost her son, perhaps her only son, whose story I had heard.

I had heard the story, I intend, from the women themselves, which is different than hearing it from anyone else. Because when you are witnessing both, the story and the woman—mother-and-son, the indissoluble dyad dissolved—you are exposed to the paradox.

Paradoxes are dangerous, tricky, more than all unforgiving.

All the women who had lost their sons... How could they be so many?

People die all the time and they all have parents. I am focusing on mothers of sons because I am one of them. I have witnessed the pain of fathers, and it is the same. But I am focusing on mothers and sons because of proximity.

I believe in proximity as I believe in paradoxes. These hurt, split and decompose. Sometimes it is needed, it's good. That (proximity) first cleans the broken edges, makes them shine either with saliva or tears. Proximity is clear-eyed. Then, proximity mends.

How many stories have I heard from mothers who have lost their (sometimes only) sons? So many that the Virgin Mary, I am sure, isn't an archetype but an a-posteriori creation, the mere summary of a way-too-common experience. Just a drop of the crimson river, sanctified as the source. Just the frame for a picture with a million faces.

*

When I drove home, still cracked, shaken by the paradox of the woman who had lost her son—death-so-alive, life-so-mortified, agony-so-raw—it was night. I was driving on the right lane of the freeway, not too fast, when my headlights hit a fawn.

Though the vision must have lasted less than a second, it was extremely distinct. Perhaps the blond color of the animal's fur, in contrast with the blackness of the asphalt, was enough to ensure perfect definition. Or it was the beauty of the beast that impressed itself, the beauty so imposing it creased my sense of sight.

The fawn rested in a curl, in fetal position. Maybe its quasi-circular shape focused my attention, mesmerizing it like a magnet would. Pale and calm on dark asphalt, the fawn was a moon. It must have been just killed because it looked fine, I thought. I didn't see blood, no interruption to the smoothness, no stain, no streak segmenting the curve of its tender body.

Of course, I can't be sure. But the fawn looked peaceful.

It looked enchanting, intact.

PAGE OF A BROKEN DIARY

1.

So why doesn't she write at her desk? Just choose a quiet moment, late night, early morning. *Madrugada*, as the Spanish say, the still hour when even planets tiptoe. Pick a moment, sit down.

No way. Entries, always incomplete, randomly land on her pad. Sentences are left in mid-air, witnesses of mysterious, dramatic breaks. Who stepped into the room? Whose was that phone call? Was there fire in the kitchen? Did the tub overflow? Sometimes there are no sentences. Sparse words cross the page, perhaps just abbreviations sided by numbers, dots, arrows, hopeful skeleton of a building to come.

And she can't sit in front of a flat surface aptly set at a proper height. She often writes in her car, the wheel functioning as an incongruous stand. On her knees, while she curls, let's say, in a corner of whatever sofa, wherever... On the floor. Oh yes, wood, carpet, concrete, tiles. Dusty or clean, shiny or matte, familiar or barely acquainted, the floor.

Why can't she sit up, for Christ sake? Answering that one isn't hard. Sitting at a table is stiff. Bodies, when they assume the position, are stuck. There's the story her elementary teacher adored, of an author who attached himself to his desk to read, learn, perhaps deliver each day the expected amount of written lines. Vain precaution. As she sits in front of a desk she is already bundled and tied. Her mind, her tongue is.

Desks and chairs are linear, perpendicular, still. Language isn't and thoughts, the matter of language, the feed, for sure aren't. They are twisting and twirling. They bend, fold, swing and oscillate. They move up and down like a thread going through fabric, back and forth like a shuttle crossing the loom. They loop, spiral and catch like wool led by the vagaries of a hook.

2.

Would a round table do? Perhaps a rotating one.

She recalls the actor sitting at her side at the Chinese restaurant. She is barely a teen, or not yet. He is a celebrity. She should be paralyzed at the mere thought of introducing herself. But who planned the seating? The point is, there's a limit to shyness, an edge. When it goes overboard it cancels itself, spilling into numbness.

She has noticed the famous man is quite kind. He looks happy. Maybe he is because the mute, skinny, astonished kid on his right is a break from aggravating adults, either flattering, flirting, or envious.

She was told the actor's a cousin of the friend who invited her to dinner. Such close kinship of his with the old family friend is quite thrilling. It emblazons her, too, with a sparkle of fame. Family of a friend of her family, oh my.

Yet all that she remembers of the guy (not a bit of his brilliant conversation, not a tasty anecdote she could turn into gossip) is that one week later he, still in his prime, is dead, having figured out the perfect suicide. He has swallowed the very number of pills needed for smoothly, painlessly passing during his sleep. Thirty, in case you wished to know. And how does such calculated gesture fit the jolly lad sitting at the round table, smartly fingering a pair of lacquered sticks?

She has never set foot into a Chinese restaurant. That's a luxury in her little town. Only actors and their kin—where, by prodigy, she suddenly belongs—peruse such facilities. She hasn't seen exotic décors before, tasted exotic food. All is new to her. The intimacy of the round table with its bold, liberal lack of hierarchy. The slick surfaces of varnished ware, the red, black and gold, spicy smells, thick sauces deep green, muddy brown. Subtle, composite flavors and tastes, teas instead of water and wine. All is new, even peanuts she rolls on her tongue like candy, daring not to chew on them. Peanuts served in a dish? She only has seen them with shells, in a paper bag, at the zoo. In a bag, like popcorn.

Yet, soon, all that she will remember of the chic Chinese joint is the Lazy Susan that keeps her mesmerized, thrilling her like a carrousel in the city square as if, yes, she were still four years old. These bowls slowly revolving, sliding by for everyone to fish out a shrimp—democratically, never mind who's first and who's last, last soon shall be first and so forth—to harpoon a green bean, scoop a spoonful of oyster dip… Though, honest, she doesn't recall shrimps or oysters, not even mushrooms or beans. Only that thing turning around like a wheel of fortune, like fate.

LORELEI

I keep wondering about the last instant of your consciousness.

The last thought? Last image, perhaps? Mental image? Most likely. You were tucked in bed. The room must have been dark.

Maybe not entirely. Twilight might have peered in, revealing silhouettes of known objects, things familiar you could identify, then complete with your imagination. The laptop on your desk, screen open. The shoe that you had kicked too far, landed against the foot of the table. The shirt hanging from the back of a chair.

Is it what last caught your attention? Just one of those trivia?

Your eyes, when you were found, were half-open. With a hint of surprise, they say. At what? Maybe pain awoke you. Just an instant fit, like a needle pocking your chest. Did it leave time for a perception, a feeling? As quick as a hiccup, they say, or a sneeze. Maybe it didn't leave time for thought, not even a seed, a bare incipit.

Perhaps, the last spark of your mind preceded that lethal spasm of a jota, a split second, an infinitesimal portion of time, yet enough for you to miss it entirely... the spasm and its full meaning, I intend.

Therefore those wide, astonished eyes registered nothing. Weren't yours anymore.

Did the last of your thoughts, then, find you asleep and dreaming? If yes, you wouldn't recall what it was.

Wait! How could you remember your very last thought, if you were awake or asleep? Be it the brightest idea, the most articulated reflection, it would be equally lost. Well, of course. So your mental activity expiring in the midst of a reverie, love, is just fine. If it were (your last thought) a pure revelation or the pearl of wisdom you had been waiting for, had you shouted it out loud for posterity to take note, you wouldn't recall it.

And it wasn't. I am sure. Nothing deep or glorious. No epiphany. How can I? What do I...

I am sure. Paradoxically it wasn't "conclusive," the last decoding spur of your brain. Last interpretation. Last act, output, last artifact that your neurons produced before your blood pump cut the juice, killing them with sudden starvation.

Did they die before you (your neurons, your thoughts)? Right after? Did your consciousness and you die together?

I don't worry too much about your last breath, your last heartbeat. Why? Not sure. Perhaps because they were "equal"… All the same and yet absolutely precious, I know. Look what happened when they ceased their faithful if monotonous labor. Everything else disappeared. I mean the diversity. The immense kaleidoscope of your world. Your words, even the unspoken ones. Look!

Don't look. I have already said it. In spite of those eyelids half-lifted, you saw nothing. Yours was the stupor of a doll, an automaton. Do not look. Back it up to the cocoon of darkness.

Let me explain. Not the darkness in which you have fallen, all dressed…

(Were you wearing pajamas of flannel, of fleece? Nights had turned icy cold, you had said on the phone. You were wearing pajamas or perhaps something more. Sweat pants and a pullover, a scarf, woolen gloves? Nights, you had said, had turned chilly.)

Leave the frigid obscurity where you have drowned head-to-toe. Go back to the porous darkness of sleep, punctuated with myriads of dots, bubbling, flickering, aerial. Stay there. Air is still coming in, going out of your nostrils. Your heart is still pumping.

Why don't I obsess about your last breath, last heartbeat? I should try to capture and hold them, claw them, clamp them in place. Why didn't you? They are, they were anonymous, sure, but invaluable. Could you have bartered a bit of brain, a slim stretch of thoughts for just another pulse? Let go of all but those bare mechanics, your vital signs?

You wouldn't have cared for those only.

I am starving for the last thing that crossed your mind, conscious or unconscious.

You were lying in bed, this I know, wearing some kind of nightgear.

Your shirt hung from the back of the chair, ready for tomorrow. The bulge, there, at chest level, was a pack of cigarettes sticking out of your pocket, half-full. Was it what you checked on, before dozing off? Your packet of fags jutting out. That angular bump, reassuring, promise of a comfy start the next morning, first smoke during breakfast, smell of fresh coffee.

That would be the case if it were I. Something trivial would kiss me goodnight. Farewell. Did I set my alarm clock? Do I have clean under-wear? Did I finish the jam? This would be the case if it were I.

But then you started dreaming.

And the last thing that crossed your mind rested behind your eye-lids, intimate and more pertinently yours than balled-up socks or the draft sneaking in from the window you should have fixed and did not.

Although, even the draft would do. A caress, a whisper.

Air. Isn't it just marvelous? Two plain vowels and a rolling conso-nant.

Rolling, running away.

A draft would be fine.

However, don't know why, I would prefer…

As if I had a say about this matter, I wish the last thing you felt, thought or dreamed were distant. A memory? A flashback? Perhaps. Distant, both chronologically and spatially. Yes, another place, other time. Childhood? Not necessarily. Past or future. Elsewhere, essential-ly.

As if, having mentally travelled far before death came in and it snatched you, you could have missed it altogether. That is my point, correct. You were gone when Miss Muerte approached. Your mind was.

Please, back up just a step or two. Please re-enter the porous dusk pocked with stars where your consciousness freely cartwheeled. Enjoy.

I am sure that you did. And where did you go?

I see cozy facades, maybe floral style, rosy-colored bricks and cast irons gates. I see pots of rhododendrons and a single plant of gardenia.

I can smell it. I can slip a bud through the buttonhole of your tux. Ah! You are dressed up! The concert must start. Here's your stick. Calmly, you advance towards the podium where the large score, wide open, awaits.

That could be a decent closing point. Hold that photogram. There.

My apologies. I shouldn't allow my imagination to oversee the labors of yours. No suggestion is needed.

Though I can't help wishing for the last spark to be somehow... evasive? Somehow fanciful, futile, therefore distracting. An aside. A phrase that you whispered in the ear of the girl sitting next to you in the theater.

You have gotten great seats by mere chance. That rich friend of yours couldn't go and he slipped you the tickets. Last moment. You had planned nothing special that night. You said yes and dug out the old dark suit from the bedroom closet, polished your pumps.

You are dreaming, of course. You are dreaming of yourself in a small town Opera House where you have unexpectedly arrived—as if in a dream?—and you are sitting by this unknown girl and all of a sudden, in the middle of an aria you actually know, could sing in your sleep...

In your dreams you sang often.

Now the girl, though, steals your attention, blotting out the scene and the music. Wait. The music stays. The scene fades away but the music, pervasive, fills the air and your pores, is everywhere.

But the scent the girl is wearing, though delicate, seems to sharpen up like a blade and you wonder what it is. You absolutely need to know. Need to turn, whisper something in her ear like, "citrus?" You are thinking of bergamot indeed.

As you turn, you notice the thread of small beads twice coiled around her neck, dark, the tint of clotted blood. Garnets are your favorite stones. You cannot help smiling. You have forgotten about what's happening on stage, though you like this melodrama a lot. Your mom used to...

But you care no more, enchanted by the deep red of garnets, live, mysterious, intense. Your eyes grow wide in the penumbra, trying to capture the shifting shades that you love. Music thunders across the rows, a wave you wish you could ride, and you really want to know what this scent is. After all it is an innocent question. Get closer. Dare asking.

GENEALOGY

I have been researching last names. Mother's first. It goes back to ancient times and has two separate roots, one signifying friend, the other god, although if I keep diving the same cluster of sound means good, which is just as well. Friends of god, friends of goodness, were they also good friends? I suspect the name only indicates a sort of gentility, and I'm slightly wary of such virtue.

A painter bore this appellative, who passed down in history. Not too famous, a portrayer of saints and madonnas in late Middle Age.

*

Then I search for Father's last name, which defines a trade and doesn't hint at nobility. I look for folks who shared it throughout the centuries. There's a well-known musician, who grew up in an orphanage, but his talent led him forwards and up. His first name was also my dad's.

I discover as well a mafioso followed by a corrupted politician. I cringe. Then a poet/union activist/railroad workers' hero evens up the score.

Wait. I just found one more item. Here.

*

It's a forest. Yes, a forest is named like my father, can you believe it? No one that I know knows this forest. It was man-made on the year Dad was born, in order to save a region from some ecologic plague. Through the forest, the area started breathing again. Those trees became its lungs. It is huge, very quiet, only hosting a small hermitage. Otherwise humans don't stride around.

No one that I know knows this forest. I'm not sure of our relationship, besides the homonymity, but I recognized it on the spot. When I saw the picture I started breathing as well, as if finding long-lost lungs. Those trees have Father's age. I suppose I could be their daughter, or niece. Likely, the forest is my aunt. We are still very close.

But unlike an aunt or Dad himself, I won't worry about losing and grieving it. The trees will survive me. Though they grow half a planet away, they'll take me when I'll pass. I will pass straight into my forest, where I namely belong.

*

Daddy's name also starts with letter F. Now it all sounds so kin, so congenial. Father. Forest. Finally. Free.

TRILOGY OF LOSS

1. At the beach

Because Mother didn't take breaks and the town was hot, I was sent to the beach with relatives whom I had never met. Wealthy people, they lived up North. That year, for some reason, they had rented a summerhouse in our area. I was four. Besides home, I had only been at my grandparents' so far. This, now, was a displacement of frightening proportions, a plunge into the unknown.

I have no memory of how I arrived to the place and who brought me there. I don't remember goodbyes. I am there already and time is absolutely still. Usually, things familiar—rooms, routes, routines—help me structure it. Clocks and calendar don't do much for me yet, but I know "when" this is, "how long" this will last, "how soon" that will occur, because of where I am and what I am doing. Here, a kind of linear flatness smooths it all.

Oh, the bungalow, how different from the turn-of-the-century building where our town apartment is perched, with its gigantic door and janitor's niche, elevators and stairs, balconies and terraces. Even counting steps while climbing to the fifth floor, landing after landing, gets me organized. But this bungalow, stretched in length, rooms like cells, all the same and barely furnished… Even the giant table where "they" reunite in the evening for endless, luscious meals imbibed with alcohol is plain, nondescript. No twisted legs or complicated underside, no long cloth transforming it into a tent where I could make my abode, nicely entertaining myself. They use rubber place mats, way more practical.

Oh, the bungalow, how different from Grandpa and Grandma's country house, full of corridors, pantries, closets, old curtains, wicker furniture sweetly crumbling away. No way to get bored while meandering through the incongruous maze, rummaging among myriads of useless residues.

Here, I said, all is linear, the bungalow, the thin stretch of sand separating it from the ocean, the expanse of pale water, the horizon. These surroundings are the spatial equivalence of eternity, a concept I am not yet fit to grasp. But it gets hold of me, nevertheless.

*

I haven't been to the sea before. I don't know how to swim. As I attempt to mimic what others do, I swallow salt water by the gallon. I sputter and spatter. I choke. No one pays close attention. Some laugh. After a week or two, an uncle visits. He brings Mama's greetings and a giant rubber swan I should ride across the waves like a wild horse. The swan helps a bit, but is kind of slippery. I'm unsteady on my saddle, fall right and left, grab the long neck that sags under frantic fingers. I keep drinking up.

I feel more at ease collecting shells in a bucket. This is a leitmotif of my stay. Afterwards, it will be all that I remember. Gathering lots, then pondering each single item. Counting, categorizing, then disposing my booty in various patterns, like a sort of calligraphy. In the backyard, close to the kitchen door. Am I mapping the void? Tracing tenuous paths. Carving marks on the sides of the wall-less prison I am in.

Now and then, the cook speaks to me through the screen door. She's the only one who tries... the one I recall. She asks me if I am homesick. What does it mean? Nostalgic, she clarifies. I am still in the dark. She needs to get on my wavelength. She comes out, bends down, looks into my eyes. Did I ever notice a knot in my throat? That is what I feel all the time.

One night, during dinner, the grown-ups look happy. Maybe it is a celebration. I notice that they are funnier and more relaxed than usual. They declare that all can eat chicken with their fingers. I guess I am included. Permissiveness is in the air.

As I grab greasy morsels and zestfully devour them, my reserve and shyness suddenly melt. For the first time I dare addressing these strangers... I ask them to play a song for me on the gramophone. I overheard the tune at different times as I was outside, tiding shells, and it caught my attention. It is called, "A shoe on your nose." Could you please put it on... the turntable, I meant. But a cousin takes off his sandal and touches his nostrils. They all laugh. I join in. They won't play the record. It is boring, they say.

And the radio, anyway, is blasting the hit of the summer. The cook always sings along with it, so I have learned it by heart without even noticing. "Here's the rain, here's the thunder," she croons, "some feel good, some feel awful."

"And some feel as they wish," I mindlessly chirp, on my four in the sand, eyes down, lining up conk shells like small, brave tin soldiers.

2. Crawl

When my grandpa died I horribly grieved him. Not only he had been a positive father figure, crucial to my development. When he died, we had just established a more mature relationship based on trust and respect, to me a portal into adulthood, a genuine initiation. Now I missed it. Growing up without it felt uninviting, and I was tempted to stop. Maybe retrace my steps? I had lost my zest for life. I felt hopeless.

In the summer I spent the day sitting on an armchair and embroidering like a little old lady. I made pillows decorated with rusty autumn leaves. One of them, the one I most liked, was for Uncle Noah, my godfather.

Noah had wanted me to be his girl's godmother as well, reinforcing the link between us. A connection of souls, rather than blood. Being a godparent or godchild in our southern tradition was a term of election, a matter of affinity unrelated to religion, though the title was given during the christening rite. Noah took his role seriously. He remembered to have an eye on me, send a note or a small present whenever he could.

He must have realized how much I was suffering after Grandpa passed. Maybe not right away, but at some point he did, and decided to shake me somehow. He would bring me to the pool, he said. I'd take swimming lessons.

That was definitely a first. My grandparents, with whom I had spent most of my childhood, lived right by the ocean but never went to the beach. And my parents didn't contemplate the seashore for vacations. Therefore I barely knew the water, and I sure couldn't swim.

I'm surprised that my dad, adamantly opposed to all kind of sports, which he deemed strictly useless and dangerously futile, conceded his permission. More surprised because I'd go to the pool, early on Saturday mornings, with three men. Adult and respectable, still three men and I was a teen-ager. An acerb, skinny one. Still, Dad came from a culture of frantic sexuophoby, casting shadows over the most innocent things.

Truly, I don't recall the slightest itch on my end. The occasion could have ben propitious to a bit of excitement, at least curiosity. I attended a girls' school. I had scant occasions to see a mixed crowd, especially a bunch of guys in their swim trunks. But that summer I was so submerged by mourning, I was anesthetized. I had lost lots of weight. I was thin, inconsistent, a ghost.

In fact, training at the pool cost me effort. I had to summon all of my strength and focus on breathing, painstakingly counting immersions, strokes, laps. I was blinded by the turquoise surrounding me, drunk with the smell of chlorine. There was room for nothing else but my straining to achieve what the instructor asked. First, conquer the fear of putting my head underwater. Then, build up tonus and endurance in my upper body. Uncle left his friends once on a while, came by to see how I was doing. He encouraged me. When the cycle of lessons expired, I could swim in style.

Swimming was the one skill I learned with orderly steps and expert instruction. I didn't have much use for it, afterwards. My life never allowed such things as vacations, and I mostly lived in mountainous areas. But whenever the occasion arose, be it a lake, a river, a pool, I felt confident thanks to Noah.

More importantly, those weeks lead me from the quagmire where I was stuck to a slight elevation. Not that high, but enough for me to turn back and realize I had moved on. No doubt, the shift happened in the water thanks to my repetitive, obedient, neat motions. Literally, I swam myself out of the deadly grip of my pain. Had Noah planned on it? Not sure. He just wanted to do something for me. Maybe that's all it takes. Did his care and affection, did love extricate me? Not love alone. Love and water.

During my adult life I have seen it happen in a movie or two, the protagonists elaborating their grief by relentless swimming. In a pool, as if the back and forth, as if linearity helped, limiting distractions, channeling, sharpening focus. I immediately recognized the feeling.

Maybe I know what the secret is. In the pool, I understood how you overcome seemingly unbearable pain. Musing, pondering, brooding don't help. Thinking turns in circles, while you have to move forwards and away by a steady repetition of motions, each bringing you a little farther. And you need to physically take those steps. No airplane, no transportation can remove you from loss. If you choose that kind of shortcut, your baggage comes along.

As I sat on a chair embroidering, hugging my pillowcase, I circled around, while I had to proceed no matter where to. I could have walked or run, true. But water is such a facilitator. It supports the body, providing encouragement, solidarity. And it offers the kind of resistance prompting you to will the next motion, carve the next foot of freedom, dig it out, claim it for yourself.

When, a quarter of a century later, Noah died, I wished I had the means to go swim. I did not, and I missed him bitterly. I hung a picture of him sitting on a beach in my living room. With a smile on his face, the blue right behind him.

3. Venice

I was almost fifteen when I went to Venice with my folks. Way too old for being excited by a family vacation, my adolescence so ripe it was on the verge of rotting. I was reaching the time when I'd take the road, say goodbye to my parents. About nine months to go. I would fly away in late summer, like the swallows. Now we were still in winter, past the Holiday season. Prices had melted already, tourists waned.

I was almost fifteen but my period hadn't yet begun and I was in agony. I attributed to my missing menstruations my androgynous looks, to my androgynous looks the lack of sex and relationships, which were all that I cared about. In addition to my despair for not becoming a woman, I internalized Father's disappointment.

My late, perhaps missing development made him feel acutely ashamed. Alas, even if it wasn't printed on my forehead, the extended family knew about my shortcoming (Mom kept aunts, uncles and cousins updated, as if my physiology were in the public domain). In particular, one of our relatives, a doctor, was frequently asked for advice. I disliked him, and his being informed especially pissed me. The poor guy worried about me. He repeatedly said that I should see a specialist, as I must have a serious dysfunction. Mom thought his apprehension unreasonable.

He was right, though. I did have something. Maybe not of the kind he intended. I was ill-adapted, a bit twisted. I was twisting myself more and more.

Venice in wintertime was a dream, but travelling with our folks wasn't fun for my siblings and me. We knew there would be drama no matter what, scenes and fights for most trivial reasons. Dad would pick ceaseless tantrums, essentially inter nos but eventually extended to a larger audience, hotel personnel and restaurant waiters, tourist guides and cab drivers.

He would regularly start off on his own, unwilling to wait for Mother and us to get ready. He'd decide where and when we should meet, but Mother would invariably get lost and we would be late. As he waited, Dad would either grow furious or leave. We would ask for something futile (some non-cultural entertainment, some tasteless banality) and he would get mad. We'd behave improperly in public and he would punish us. Mother would be upset and whine. They would argue, guilt about their disharmony weighing down on our shoulders. Angry silence would follow.

In addition, we would visit monument after monument and it would be all. No acquainting fellow travelers, no distractions, no fun. No bar sitting or window licking. Only culture, and religion of course. Churches would be on the menu, and we would attend Mass wherever we went.

Still, Venice in winter was beyond gorgeous, and I did what I used to do in such situations. I daydreamed. I took in the wonderful sights and the enchanting moments, tuning up to the smallest parcel of beauty, sipping every inch of landscape, shifting shade of water and sky, murmur, scent, then I shared them with a fictional mate, an invented lover. As I summoned him at my side, reveling in our amorous duet, my flesh-and-blooded company faded away.

Yes, the town was spectacular, veiled by the softest fog, full of palpitation. I could have savored the magic and be contented. Something, though, transformed the vision into a nightmare.

On the second night of our stay my young sister, nine years old, got her period. Way too early. Mom became extremely anxious, besides busy explaining, directing, helping the astonished girl. Mother was concerned because Sister was small, and as she got menstruated she might stop growing. Such prospective catastrophe made Mother panic, and she talked about it non-stop.

As we walked through serpentine alleys, crossed small bridges arched over eerie canals squeezed among fabulous buildings, pastel colored, laced with exquisitely wrought marble friezes, Mother ceaselessly yapped about the same thing. Not with Sister, who for god's sake shouldn't share her worries. But with me, over and over.

I didn't reply, as a strange feeling gradually took hold of me. I was sliding down, deep and low. Backing up. Shrinking. Retrograding. Retracting. Not in infancy (I certainly wasn't a child anymore) but in a sort of neutrality, a state of indifference. A limbo. Suddenly I had fallen off the expected trajectory leading me towards a defined female identity. Sister, six years younger, had surpassed me. Sis? Still yesterday, it seemed, I was babying her, substituting Mom who was overloaded with work and responsibilities. I had been asked to take care of the new child, and I had responded with enthusiasm.

Now the little one whom I had fed, dressed up, helped to the bathroom, technically was in state of producing progeny. She could become a Mom, believe it or not, while I couldn't. Would I ever? The question hadn't yet formulated itself. Now it choked me. I remember a pang, a sharp cramp of pain. Alas, not in my uterus. A bit higher, in my heart, a less demonstrative organ. As we kept strolling, a cloud of despair submerged me.

Sure, I couldn't openly tell I was envious, not even to myself. I mortally was. I sure couldn't cry, "What about me?" and yet all of my cells were chanting those words. But crying them out loud would have been childish, and I wasn't a child anymore.

As evening neared we took the last boat to the Island of the Dead, the actual cemetery, so frequently reproduced in paintings. How absolutely haunting, as it slid forwards to meet us, quickly magnified, towering above us. As I said, the weather was perfect, gray, wet and mournful. Do I remember a tolling bell out of nowhere?

I can't truly retrace what I thought when we set foot in the graveyard, if I wished to be left there, call it quits. I know I linked that site at once with my internal state of decomposition. The décor fit me perfectly.

Suddenly, I had lost faith that things would straighten themselves. What I was waiting for, I realized, might never occur. How did I reach such conclusion? Was it Sis beating me to the finish line? Was it Mom, pouring her concerns over me as if I...

As if I didn't exist. That small graveyard, alone like a diamond, ringed by lapping waves singing litanies, was peaceful. It felt heavenly and my life looked like hell. I don't recall any combativeness, or the faintest hope. Maybe the sun would rise at some point, but now I couldn't think of it. Venice was just a bloody crepuscule.

THE RIDE

Yusuf tells me I'm beautiful. A quick glance into the rear mirror and then: "My eyes are still good," he mumbles. Enough to appreciate my looks, though he got older since he last saw me, alas. I did not, he implies.

Sometimes he even spoils me, stating I didn't change and then specifying I'm pretty. If it sounds redundant, it isn't. I could be young looking and ugly. I am grateful for his profuse kindness.

He no more mentions my likeness to a movie celebrity. No need. Such initial remark eased our introduction, long ago.

I see Yusuf about once a year for about half hour. Don't exactly see him, just spot his eyes in the mirror. Recently he has taken on turning towards me while driving, for conversation sake. Am I scared? Not a bit. I trust him entirely. And the town, when we meet (always the same hour) is clear like a cloudless sky. Only, more black than blue, neon signs and car lights shining against asphalt. Our town in the wee hours is a parody of itself, a postcards booklet that you can flip with your thumb. Not quite real, and its eeriness fits my mood.

We go from downtown to the airport. The ride usually takes an eternity. Now we could make it in twenty minutes, should we wish. But we stretch it to a more leisurely pace, still fast, rather elegant.

Yusuf had to choose between night birds and daytime traffic jams, here notoriously insane. Tough pick, but he made it. He works nights. And I only fly at dawn when, homebound, I leave my motherland.

*

Father met Yusuf accidentally and then he kept his phone number, wishing to directly call on occasion. Dad is old-fashion-personable, and extremely so. He likes forging relationships with the folks he deals with, as it naturally occurred in the village. He always visits the same market boots. He addresses vendors by their first names, adding some quirky jokes, his very idea of familiarity. Then he asks for the impossible, the one thing they didn't carry, today, or he loudly critics the quality of a product. He intends to be tickling, gently provoking, but he sounds like a little nasty old man. You'll suppose he is hated. For some reason he manages to be adored.

Yusuf loves Dad. When the cab pulls to the curb, in front of the building, Father is unfailingly there. He always beats me downstairs (well, he takes the lift), sneaking out when I'm in the restrooms or checking my bags. He absolutely wants to pay for the ride. It is a goodbye present that, we know, might become a farewell one. So he sees Yusuf first, in private.

"All done," they exclaim with a blink as soon as I appear. Mother holds my arm, sad and teary as the occasion demands. The air is crisp, even in summer. Streets deserted, noise muted. Dad wears dark. All buttoned up in his navy coat, beret-basque on his head, he blends with the surroundings. I hug him tight, without words. Same with Mother. I'm not sure in which order.

They stand motionless while the car takes off and I stare at their figures, tiny, uncannily stilled as if petrified, until they disappear. I know they will take each other's arm now, then stagger with cautious steps, seeking balance. They will make sure to lock the street door behind them. They will return to bed. At least Mother will.

Father might make coffee and then, in his studio, comfy in his armchair with the portable desk, he might begin to work.

*

Yusuf admires Dad's education and knowledge, which he deems outstanding. Dad must have dazzled him, for sure, during their first ride. Dad is also a simple folk, one who came from the village and, though he went to college, didn't lose his popular roots or learned how to conceal them. Dad still scents the stable, so to speak, and conversely all of Yusuf's daughters graduated, got prestigious careers. They have become Father's peers. Therefore, a bridge joins driver and passenger.

Yusuf tells me his late father would have been exactly Dad's age. He had great tenderness and respect, he says, for his old man. He clearly associates the two figures. Unavoidably, he extends his filial sentiment

138

to this casually met aging guy. See how little it takes.

Once, while commenting about meaningful encounters making up for the drabness of the night crowd, Yusuf candidly avows this scene always fills his heart. He is talking of my parents and me biding good-bye, farewell. Daddy's ritual of pre-paid fare. Our hugs in the dark. The stilled figures. All of it, he adds, perhaps to dispel a slight ambiguity, saddens him of course. But also fulfills him, he insists.

Where you see separation you see love. True? Love coats the edges of departures. It spills out of the crack like foam fringing the groove a boat cuts through water.Where you see farewells you see love, its foot-print, its shadow, in one of its rare manifestations. Presumptions. I'm sure love, its trace, is what momentarily nurtures Yusuf's heart.

How much love can you spot downtown, at night, in the streets? Not a lot, says Yusuf.

*

We talk horses, a passion of his I can share. Son and grandson of horse traders, Yusuf rode since he was five. For a while he has matched his cabdriver job with a small horse business. Two or three animals, in the glorious days. One or two. Then one. He gave lessons of equitation, organized beginner excursions in the desert. It was what he lived for, the bright side.

Only recently, after a bad fall, Yusuf gave up riding. He doesn't re-gret it too much. He has a lifetime of memories, and I am never tired of listening. His equestrian adventures enthrall me. Is it because they contrast with this cab ride, this mechanic fugue among buildings? No. There is resemblance, indeed. I'm experiencing a gush of freedom on this back seat, out of time, between places. Yusuf's pictures of wild gallops fit my present state, fill my heart or rather expand it just as my goodbye hugs filled his, minutes ago.

Once, while visiting Egypt with his family, Yusuf rode an Arabian horse for the first time. "Don't say I can ride," he whispered to his wife and kids, "or they'll give me the worst, the unmanageable." He mount-ed carefully, almost religiously.

He had already tried Spanish horses, so sensitive you can feel tendons start, muscles tense as if they were your own. You commune with your mount in a perfect fusion. But Arabian horses, in a way, are the opposite. They glide smooth, horizontal. Once you are steadied and tight you need to give up control. They are so built they become a vector, a quiet arrow espousing its self-secreted momentum.

"Does it feel like flying?" I ask. Yes it does. Yusuf never forgot that first ride. "Arabian horses," locals say, "are born by the wind." Yusuf whispers the words reverentially, as if they were crystals, pearls, precious stones. "It is true," he states, eyes lost in the rear mirror.

I believe him.

THE WINDOW

Then I'd run to the window. Square. Press myself against its marble sill. The softness of my body was met, secured, contained by that margin.

That wasn't enough, though, to control my brothers and me. As a matter of fact, the windowsill caused our irresistible wish to climb, then sit on it sideways. It was confortable for our size, like a high sturdy bench. A change from the carpet or the bare floor (carpets where removed in summer). A change from our little chairs in painted wood, laminated with formica.

There were not enough chairs. I don't know why we outnumbered them. We couldn't all sit around the small table (also laminated with formica, corners chipped and worn out) for our playing activities. No. There had to be fight about it. Someone won, someone lost. Someone went to squat on the bed that of course we used as a multitasking piece of furniture, morphing at our demand. Someone pouted under the bed perhaps, discontent with the outcome of the struggle. One of us was especially fond of such dramatic gestures. Or indeed he liked the penumbra, the coziness, the snug feeling of that peculiar abode.

Once in a while, I said, we perched on the windowsill sideways. The most fortunate rested their back against the lateral walls, but we usually didn't fight for such privilege. It must have been the effect of the altitude. I've omitted to say, but you have guessed, that two massive bars blocked the opening. Tall enough not to be climbed over. Low enough for no kid to slide under.

We lived at the fifth story of an old building. Underneath was a street, with its flow of cars and passers by that we loved to peek at from our observatory. No, we didn't comment on them. We were young and not very articulate. There was nothing to say. The show mesmerized us without need for words. It operated its magic on each of us, individually. Which magic I can't tell.

Only intentionally, and of course sitting as described, we could catch the vertiginous sight of people down there. I didn't always need it.

Sometimes it was enough to stand on a little stool, squeeze against the edge, watch what I could still see. Meaning, the fifth and fourth floor of the opposite building, the façade, the interiors as well. I caught glimpses of furniture, people, gestures, always sliced by the window frames, always without beginning or end. Good enough. Fantasy did the rest.

No sense of intrusion accompanied my amusement, of an innocent nature. I didn't know what morbid curiosity was. I had no idea of gossip. I looked in (no one said I shouldn't) as if leafing through a book with delightful pictures, square and evenly distanced. Some complete, some halved, some temporarily crossed. Just like those Christmas calendars with (indeed) little windows to be opened one at a time, each hiding a cute illustration. I was used to such calendars, and the building in front was just a larger version, more exciting, of the very same magic.

No words labeled the images. The story was missing. I provided it.

Still my favorite window, which I seldom accessed, was on the other side of the corridor. It belonged to my father's office, a sancta sanctorum where I wasn't supposed to set foot but sometimes I did. That one window allowed an enchanting view of the river, blond, like in a rhyme Father taught me when I was two.

Blond, green, brown as well, the river had many colors. Seagulls inhabited its shores. They perched on the bridge, on the streetlights, busy, noisy. Great companions, the seagulls. Also, barges passed by. Some were anchored as permanent residences for fishing or boating clubs. One of them was bright yellow, a small cottage with a pointed roof. I couldn't precisely see it (too far) but it fascinated me, I suppose, because of its flashy color.

When I even so rarely sneaked to that particular window, providing the greatest deal of evasion, my gaze eagerly sought the yellow casino. To me it was a landmark. Who knows why some things become a pole of attraction, a key allowing access to the whole? First, my eye would fasten itself to the little house. Reassured, it would lift, explore, embrace the view of sensuous hills and the myriads of roofs, domes, steeples, terraces. The pines, weaving into the tapestry of brick and stone their tufts of dark green, their balsamic presence.

The casino only occupied part of the barge that also comprehended a garden, potted of course. I thought I could detect colorful vases filled with succulents, flowers, perhaps miniature palms. That's what I recognized, my botanic notions being limited. I also thought I saw a little fountain, a sort of marble basin. I couldn't tell if it was oval or triangular, my geometry being in progress as well. I could see a flicker that suggested water in it, the whole concept somehow stupefying, overwhelming. A pool, floating? A little lake on a river?

I saw a silvery flash, I said, but essentially something turquoise or blue. Shiny and bright like a precious stone. Perhaps the fountain was lined with tiles. That would match the majolica planters, the entire setting reminiscent of Andalusia or Greece, a Moorish extravaganza. But of course I missed all these references.

With the blue I was obsessed. My eye, now oblivious of yellow, sought it first. I craved that shiny dot, oval or triangle, who cared. How I wanted to sit on the edge, dip my hand into the water! I believed there could be coy fishes. Had to. Only, I couldn't see them unless I sat by, which I wished with sharper and sharper longing. Not of the morbid kind... I said sharp, like a needle. Like a high C only the best soprano can hit.

I also thought, by a later conceived hypothesis, there could be turtles, bronze colored, starkly contrasting with the azure ground. Small turtles. You could lose your mind over them. I so wanted to sit on the fountain edge and try touching, lightly, one of those little turtles.

Then, one day I thought that I spotted a girl by the fountain. I could tell by the dress, pale pink. I couldn't make out its shape, but the color was revealing enough. No boy would ever wear it. That was not my favorite shade. I liked other tones, fuchsia, lobster. Throbbing hues, less ethereal or sweet.

But the idea, I mean the sight of the girl was thrilling. I detected a very long braid, neatly drawn against the light expanse of the dress, when she showed her back to me and turned towards the pool. Yes, she turned and she bent, certainly about to caress whatever fish or turtle was there. And the lotus flowers... that I couldn't see because they were hiding, shy, squeezed against the edges. I adored lotus flowers, which I had seen in pictures only. In books.

Her long braid swung around the girl like a whip. I had two of them and shorter. Then she stood still a while, facing my direction. I could guess the shape of her face, not her features. Her pose made her look pensive. It seemed as if she stared at me. Did she? Could she see me from where she was? Make out my head and torso in the cutout of Dad's office window? Higher, so much higher than where she was? I had no clue.

But she seemed to look at me and I responded to her gaze, telling her without words an awful lot of things. The exchange wasn't verbal, therefore difficult to reconstruct or recall. Meaningful nonetheless.

She appeared again, but quite randomly. I consequently didn't expect her, not truly. She did not become my secret friend, perhaps due to her volatility that, believe me, I could sense. I'm not sure she turned in my direction again. Perhaps she did not.

Honestly, I don't recall when she vanished and how. Probably by mere rarefaction. I saw her seldom, then barely, then I stopped seeing her, that's all. Maybe she had come visit her grandma, let's say, for a season. Maybe she was a stranger and strangers, I learned, come and go. I forgot all about her, our brief telepathic call notwithstanding.

At some point, when my brothers and I went to kindergarten, then school, when someone finally brought us to the park in the afternoon, I forgot the fountain as well. Windows lost their fascination, their charm. They became things you open to allow fresh air in, nothing else. I now could read books with words, entire stories, and I could understand them. I was told that people had separate, private lives. My hair was cut short.

IN THE WATER

The wide cistern where the main supply of water is stored has a strange name. Later she will know it is derived from Arabic, as are all eerily-sounding words, in the island. The huge tank is mysterious and scary. Almost nothing else frightens her. Neither the stable where the bull is kept, nor the pigsty, though its dwellers can scream loud and sharp especially on slaughtering days. Neither the moonless night, nor getting lost on the hills after sunset. Not vipers, with their snappy bifurcate tongue. Not thunderstorms, but the *gebbia* has something about it, like a buried secret, a mute threat.

Its concrete walls are grey, nude, severe. From the outside it looks a sad bunker, but if you climb the stairs etched in its sides you realize water fills it to the top. Imagine a giant cube full of liquid, rising towards the sky. Think of one of those walls giving up. It won't. That is why the construction is bulky, solid, secure. Water comes to the edge, olive, dense, impenetrable. The green hue and oily consistence make it mischievous, mortuary. This water is grieving.

Or indeed it is murderous. It has been clearly spelled, no secret. A boy has fallen inside and he has drowned. It will happen if she doesn't pay attention. She does. Water has gulped the boy. Killer depths. The opaque stillness of the surface, the inability of seeing what is below, appraising how far is the bottom, slightly trouble her.

Yet of course she can't resist playing at the edge, where she spends long hours because of the frogs. They are emerald jewels. They swim. Do they? They hop and jump so close to her hand she can catch them, fearlessly grabbing their cool slippery bodies. Such a thrill! Each capture makes her feel brave and competent. She relishes holding them in the cavity of her palm, then releasing them. What else should she do? She can't bring them home like blackberries or flowers. She can brag about it.

Frogs are only to be found in the *gebbia*. Smaller basins, culverts, irrigation channels spread all over the orchards aren't favored by their kind. Yet they are only the official reason of her visit. Rather the conscious one. She is aware, though slightly, of the charm the column has on her, the square pillar of uncertain function built at the very center of the tank.

She likes its forlorn unreachability, rigorous geometry, more than all the tuft of vegetation (a small cactus, a palm, a bunch of bamboo reeds) that makes it appear like an island. A grey little world of concrete, inaccessible. How does it crystallize her attention, tickling her ear like a background drone. How it calls her, deaf murmur in the distance.

Still, what most attracts her to the water edge is danger itself, with its irresistible magnetism. Because only if you look at peril from close, again and again, you'll come to realize it is a meek companion simply asking for a little respect, a nod of acknowledgment. In exchange for your discrete frequentation and prudent behavior, danger gives you great gifts delivered in shy, tiny installments. Makes you strong. Makes you free. She doesn't know yet.

Grandpa has introduced her to frogs as well as he has acquainted her with vipers and larger yet less dangerous snakes. He has taught her how to catch lizards into a noose made with a blade of grass, and then walk them around like dogs on a leash. He has given her sound, wise, precise instructions for whenever she'd wander alone. He has told her the habits of insects, birds, mammals, the nature of plants and rocks. How to interpret the sky, clouds, wind, bark on tree trunks.

There's another dangerous place on the property, he has said, where she is supposed to behave. It's a hole in the hillside, the opening of a cavern. He has told her not to get in and she obeys, though temptation creeps over her body. But she manages to stop by the entrance, made almost invisible by accumulated debris, by a mound of slippery rock on which a fig tree has sprouted, partially obstructing the access. She should carve her way among its crooked, curvy, tentacular branches in order to proceed. The fig tree winks at her like a Jiminy cricket. It reminds her of her promise of sensible, prudent compliance. It would squeal on her, perhaps. Perhaps, too late.

The tunnel was originally shaped like a horseshoe, with two entrances/or/exits. If the soldiers found one of them, with some luck they might not spot the other, and then... What a silly thought. Soldiers had nothing to do with it. The obvious reason for the two holes was fear of a landslide. In case bombs would cause the hill to collapse and block one entrance, they all would run the opposite way, trying not to be buried alive, munched up by a cold jaw of dirt and stone.

That is what occurred indeed. One entrance collapsed. Only, years after the war had ended. But she should be alert! The other opening might, will close up as well. Still a pull, like a tide, irresistibly makes her climb the irregular slope, linger under the sappy, sticky fig leaves. How she wishes to see the little chamber! Oh my. Decades later she will vividly recall it. She'll be sure she has gone inside, probably accompanied. Her memory is too neat not to reproduce real data.

And yet, no. Reason dictates that no sensible grown-up would have entered the tunnel, especially not ventured into the small room, hidden deep in the guts of the mountain, far removed from daylight. A tiny cot was inside it, Grandma said, where she laid down her third son, five or six years old, ill with typhus and burning with fever. Why did she have to conceal him in such remote corner? In her words it sounds like protection. Was it fear of contagion instead?

She could swear she has been in the room, a minuscule cell with dirt walls, dirt floor, and she has seen the cot. The remains of it, a pile of wood slates, the bare skeleton of a bed come undone. Of course it isn't possible. And the wood would have been rotten by then. Positively, no one ventured into the shelter. This must be a fruit of her imagination, fleshing up Grandmother's enthralling tale. She has never, ever seen the dungeon where the sick boy has lain, night after night.

In the walls of the tunnel, all along, there are little indents. Little shelves where candles were put, the only furniture. Children, women, sick, cripple and old would squat on the floor, the most fortunate resting their back against rock. Many of them, as many as they could fit, gathering from the village, the farms. They would sit in silence, waiting for the plane raids to subside.

She has seen piles of charred planks on the ground though, for good. But that was the little house at mid-hill, a shed where Father stopped to read the paper when (once on a while) they hiked to the top all together, as a family thing. Dad obliged but not for too long. He wasn't fond of exercise. At mid-way he gave up, opened a folding chair he had carried along together with the papers. The shed was his landmark.

Though neither he nor anyone ever entered it, though she didn't know what it was for, she loved the small cabin where Dad was lost, then found on their way down. She was flabbergasted, the day when she saw a pattern of smashed bricks, tiles, burned timber instead of it. All had fallen straight down, drawing a two-dimensional version of the previous volumes. Is it what fire does? Is it what melting means? This kneeling, meekly reclining.

Fire has gulped the cabin, leaving this brisk void in its place. She can feel the wind from the sea claiming yet another playground. She can see it, the wind, summersaulting unbound, enthusiastic and arrogant. Where will Father rest now, on their way to the top? Alas, he stops coming, tired of these vain childish strolls. He only needed an opportunity for his final desertion. He found it.

At the very top of the hill there's a locust tree, the most elevated specimen of vegetation around. Its daring and solitude give it an eerie majesty, as for an ancient hermit of sorts. Beyond the tree is a fence. What does barbed wire do up here, separating two contiguous slices of wilderness?

She understands it marks property limits, signaling the end of the world she is allowed to explore. She accepts more than truly comprehending. In a recess of her mind contradiction arises, itching, stubborn, disturbing. Exploration, she ponders, should be inherently endless. Exploration doesn't steal, harm or hurt. At the top of the hill, past the locust tree, a crooked, bunched up yet not less impassable fence clumsily cuts the trail, embossing the hill with a long irregular scar. She has to retrace her steps before these Pillars of Hercules where, she is sure, even birds hesitate, turn in circles, get lost.

Grandpa had a dream, Mother told her. Mom used to picture her father as a melancholy man who had given up wishes, aspirations, desires. Well who hasn't, at least partially? By the way, at the time she was granted the confidence she already knew there were dreams in Grandfather's past. At least two.

One, the easel, the canvases and the set of oil paints she had found in the attic. To whom did these belong? No one claimed them. The attic was off-limits during her childhood, separated from the house by unfinished restructuring work, only accessible if a ladder was pulled across, a drawbridge she furtively crawled upon.

In the abandoned attic the easel stood like a monument, sporting a thick coat of gluey dust and an incomplete charcoal sketch, delicate, evanescent outlines of a turn-of-the-century mansion, a faint color of rust. Each time she accessed, unpermitted, the forgotten sanctum, her eyes drank in the drawing, her heart squeezed with nostalgia not sure of what. Yes, he had painted in his youth, and that wasn't all.

In the cellar, after he was dead, she found a shelf of Russian books filled with red and black illustrations. As she mentioned her discovery to relatives, the anecdote came up he had been oh-so-briefly a communist, then an anarchist but just momentarily, promptly resuming his land-ownerish, aristocratic notions. Just a spur of juvenile foolishness. But that wasn't all.

Last but not least was his archeological passion, the obsessive hope that he would discover something some day. After all Greek, Egyptian, Carthaginian and Roman conquerors had claimed this land in turns, these sweet hills overseeing the blue. He did find, Mother said, shards, fragments. Not sure what, but evidence of a larger something. He could have pursued, excavated. He got scared instead. Permits. Licenses. City. Government. Taxes and regulations. Perhaps expropriation? Maybe loosing the land, god forbid.

Not only he didn't dig. He decided to build over the hot spot something large, heavy, unmovable. Something muddy, opaque, mysterious and mute. The wide tank, devourer of children, immature aspirations, young dreams. The tall *gebbia* where emerald frogs thrived, uncaring and mindless, where the girl liked to play, mildly aware of some obscure evil lurking underneath.

Perhaps, only regret.

THE SAME

Iwas three or four years old, spending whole afternoons by the water pipe. Just an open groove of concrete meant for irrigation, it spread throughout the orchards, branching off in intricate nets. To me it was a labyrinth, a freeway leading everywhere, a tool of discovery.

I sat there, for how long? Time didn't make sense. I sat there enchanted, my hand brushing the green, muddy stream as majestic as a Mississippi or a Nile, which I didn't know existed.

I was thrilled by the occasional leaf falling in, then being carried along. Following its course toward unrevealed destination was bliss. I saw it slide away, suddenly accelerate, hesitate then rush. I pursued it until darkness came and a grown-up found me, promptly returning me to the house, grandparents, and dinner.

Half a century later I kneel by a flowerbed, carefully pulling weeds. My hand plunges into the river of grass, gravel, dirt, my torso inclined. My eyes lost in contemplation of a single corner of earth, I'm entirely oblivious. I breathe in the peace nature pours over me, erasing all noise.

NIGHTWATCH

1.

Father, are you sleeping? I am not sure. You look like you might have dozed off, but I know better. You must be thinking instead, in that thick manner of yours, so dense it makes like a curtain, severing the world away.

Not only you are awake. I am sure, though you haven't uttered a word, you have something to tell me. You wish to communicate. You have turned towards me even so slightly, trusted your chin my way in guise of a nod, and your eyes are piercing.

Well, you could be more explicit, you know. You aren't that frail yet, that sick or exhausted. But you are so used to be understood, then obeyed, with minimal effort... Such an embedded habit.

As you finally start your sentence, my hand rushes towards your head for a spontaneous caress. My fingers draw the line of your nape. My palm lingers, cupping the base of your skull as if to support it. It's a comforting feeling, for me at least, and so natural, I wonder why.

Suddenly I realize the meaningfulness of such gesture must have something to do with what's under your skin, right there. Cerebellum? Brain stem? Hidden reservoir of things precious and mighty. Your emotions, your affects, your memories.

Most of all your memory, and another epiphany comes my way. Myths about Pandora's vase or those coffers, purses, baskets we find in fairy tales, magically refilling themselves, spitting out gold or food aplenty, like bottomless wells...

All such fantasies must be born by the simple evidence of this thing we host among cranial bones, a teacup of matter where an unbelievable quantity of data are stored. Such a tiny place, such immense contents.

And isn't it strange how this plethora of images, narratives, notions with correlated feelings vanishes and reappears, gets collapsed, zipped, lyophilizated, to emerge at a given moment like a print in the darkroom?

Maybe that is where the idea of god originates. Invisible, knowing it all, so is our memory. Also random, capricious, mysterious. Dad, I hold your skull almost reverently, fingertips brushing your nape.

"When I won't be around any more," you say, "who…

You pause, either distracted or pondering. I finish the sentence. "Who will take care of me?" Your eyes blink. You keep silent. I repeat, hammering the final question mark. You answer in a rush, as if time had briskly run over. "You," or rather, in our mother tongue, "*tu*."

The short monosyllable hits me but doesn't hurt me. Does it wake me up? I thought I was sufficiently alert. It reaches me like a stone or a bullet. I had never realized how solid and compact a small pronoun can be. T, an unforgiving letter, definite and inflexible, ultimate like the following vowel. "You/*Tu*," a last commandment. Received. Do not worry. I'll be in charge of myself. Now rest.

Crows fly across the early evening sky, briefly dotting the paleness behind the open window. A fan buzzes on the bed stand. Dad is always hot, no matter the season. High metabolism and quick blood circulation.

There's a book on the bed stand. There is always a book in the proximity of Father. I know, as soon as I'll say goodbye he will slowly turn, grab the volume and open it at the very page where he left it, as he exactly recalls the last paragraph, sentence, the last word he read. Memory never failed him. So prodigious.

Yet, I wonder. What will those extra packages of cognizance do for him? Does he need them at this point? Clearly he does. He will feed yet another thought, another sentence to the secret bank of his mind until the minute he passes. Then? What happens when in a blink, a split second, consciousness disappears?

2.

Now Father is falling. He seems to lose his balance more and more often. Not sure how he manages to end up flat on his back, each time, perfectly supine, neither I know why such posture strikes me so much. Maybe its straightness and peculiar composure have a surreal tinge.

Father barely whines, not quite demonstratively. No one hears him. I almost bumped on him the first and second time. Now I cautiously advance through the corridor, at night, when most of the falls occur.

Every time I found him, of course, he wore his pajamas. He must have been bound to the bathroom or the kitchen. When I asked what had happened he did not provide explanations. He always slights irrelevant questions, rather sparing his breath.

Here. Once more he lies still. No, not like a corpse. Like a rag doll, the pale fabric of his nightwear melting with the candor of his head. Mute, besides that tranquil lament. Then, with a brisk, almost impatient sigh he reaches out, lifts his hand still emblazoned with his wedding ring. As our fingers cross, I steady myself while he gathers his strength and pulls up.

A sound. Yet another sigh? A whine? Rather a gasp but shrill, sharp, like the cry of a small animal escapes him. Maybe he doesn't realize. I do. I cringe. He is now on his feet.

Speaking of which, I am spellbound. He is wearing a pair of dance slippers, pale pink, the color of flesh. Old, and falling apart. Where did he possibly, and why… This is so much unlike him I feel dizzy, as it happens when you notice something incongruous and your brain can't wrap itself around it.

As he sees me look down in disbelief, he chuckles. Again, the sound of his giggles has a shrill note mixed in, like a wheezing, or as if he's about to choke. Briefly, then it is gone.

Boldly, he sets off towards the bedroom but his whole body wavers, his balance uncertain, and he shuffles with painstaking effort, as if someone had smeared the pavement with glue.

I hang around him like an awkward ghost, clumsy shadow, daring not to support him yet ready to catch him, at least try, should he crash like a quill hit by an invisible ball. Slowly, we inch our way to our destination, covering those ten feet of cold tiles during what most resembles a suspension of time.

In no time then, and virtual immobility, in the syrupy, murky light, a blend of the dim ceiling lamp and the first shreds of dawn peering through the back door, we land. He drops on his bed, his legs buckling below him. Seated, with bust erect but perfectly expressionless, his sap seems to have left him entirely, a stringless puppet. As I silently watch him I start working on a smile.

The dance slippers have fallen upon the carpet against which their color veers, now more beige than rosy. They look even more battered, sad. They have lost their surreal fairy-talish flavor. Neutrally, as if pushed by the most generic curiosity, I ask: "Where did you find them?"

He is staring at the wall, straight ahead, and does not seem to hear me. I know better. His brain is quickly processing my question. Should it be tossed into the useless pile or does it deserve an answer, which in such case should be the most economic and functional? He imperceptibly thrusts his chin towards a closet squeezed in a corner, from where he clearly dug out his footwear.

I am not surprised, as I imagine the collection of trivia Mom must have amassed on those shelves, with no ratio besides the erratic motions of her... memory. She threw nothing away. She accumulated random relics in all forms of containers, picturesque formations of tokens and artifacts from the past. Mom. I confess, when she was alive, I seldom caressed her nape, probably because her permed curls were in the way.

Once more, my gaze is magnetized by the ballet shoes. Irresistibly. They might have been mine, after all. Perhaps. I am struck by a hint of familiarity simultaneous to a sense of remoteness, alienness. Again, for a split second I am not sure of...

Wait. As I got distracted Dad has turned around, pulled his legs onto the mattress. Still seated, he now drags himself backwards towards the pillows, awkwardly and with seemingly enormous strain. He looks serious and once more the shrill whine escapes him. He does not realize or he doesn't care.

I lean forward to help, but he frowns and imperiously shakes his head. Once he is comfortably placed he turns on his bed lamp, bright like a fog breaker. Shiny beams hit the cover of the book already in his hands, shaky fingers fumble through it while a pencil rolls over the blankets, to the side. Dad's left hand blindly prods to recuperate the lost lead, his right grasps the thin ribbon marking the page, his brow knit in concentration.

Clearly, I am now redundant. I should go. Wait. Suddenly our conversation—our synthetic exchange—of a week ago comes to mind. How he wondered about who'd take care of his daughter after... How he ordered me to be in charge of myself. I can't avoid giggling. Look at him, proud, self sufficient, needing nothing at all. Why do I bother?

Mindlessly or perhaps to prolong the moment, postpone exit, I exhale: "Aren't you going to sleep?" He doesn't hear me. Well, of course he does. As I make it for the door, my eyes still on him, I see he's working on a smile. Incredible. "No, sweetheart." Is it right? "No, sweetheart," his voice fluid, no wheeze. He has fully recovered his wind. Only, someone must have turned the volume all the way down.

I listen carefully. The early hour is quiet. Birds are Dad's only competitors. "I can't, now. I need to read a few pages." There's a mellowness in his tone—is it peace?—as his fingers point at the door, wave me away.

BOOK OF HOURS

When I awoke Dad already sat at his desk, staring vacuously at nothing, twisting between index and thumb a felt pen, ultra-fine, fit for his minute hieroglyphs. Dad handwrote (never learned how to type) on a stack of paper (never used notebooks). In the summer he wore a pair of boxers, that's all and he couldn't care less. He sat there half-naked, oblivious. He had swallowed a cup of coffee at four. At six he would go to Mass. On his way home he'd buy the newspapers, then slouch on his armchair and read. Mother soon would join him. They would start arguing about whatever first came to mind. And the day would begin.

But when I awoke, at five, Dad sat at his desk, pen or pencil in hand. He did not hear or see me until he lifted his gaze. I scared him. He jumped on his chair, then he smiled, which he otherwise never did. A brief flash of complicity lit his brow as if, briskly, he had recalled the two of us had something in common. A same vein of wildness, same need for quiet solitude. A same pondering bug devouring our brains. Was he proud of me for a second?

Wishful thinking. Though our eyes met and his lips curled, Dad still didn't see me. I was a walking mirror, catching the magic moment when doubtlessly Father was handsome. A halo surrounded him, I swear, a ring of purple someone said they saw around me, much later. When I wrote, painted, played music. When I did what I was meant for.

Like Father did, daily, at the break of dawn.

LEAVING

1. Dying

Since my younger brother died an abrupt death, at the break of dawn, on St. Valentine Day, I die every night. I mean I prepare myself. Because why should I survive him? I don't see a reason. Therefore my existence, which always was kind of inconsistent, has become improbable. Frankly, each day is an exception. Each evening a vigil. Each night a possible grave.

He died of a congenital aneurism, they stated. If so, chances are I'll share the opportunity. I have had the same mild, un-worrisome symptoms he had, for years. His apparently were prelude to the briskest conclusion. Why shouldn't mine? I have reported them to my doctor, a bit carelessly. I shall do some checks in due time. Soon. Truth is, my state doesn't suggest emergency. His didn't either.

He died instantaneously. Certainly, they said, without noticing. His body was composed, his face peaceful. His hand seemed to have hinted at pushing away the edge of the blanket. Did he feel anything? Was he suddenly warm? Did he wish to get up, seek a glass of water? His face, they said, was peaceful.

Each night since, before I close my eyes I say my farewells. Because why should I stay if he left? For a fact, if I pass it will not be terrible, because I'll be unaware of my absence. For a fact, whoever will suffer for the loss of me will recover at last, because life goes on. Therefore, all I have to deal with is this moment's subtle, ineffable sadness, which is only related to leaving. Leaving it all.

I recall having pondered this quite a lot in a fictional, artificial way, a few decades ago. I was acting a prisoner in a play, and I was about to take my life in my cell. After my decision was made, there were quiet yet meaningful moments when my expression should convey my forthcoming departure from the world. I had rehearsed the scene over and over until I felt it was solid. The device I had found was to picture a familiar landscape filled with things, places, beings I loved. Then I'd see the landscape gradually recede, with an almost imperceptible motion. A smooth fading, a loss of contour, details blurring themselves. Because nothing was abrupt, despair had no place as it is a fast, flashy feeling. Sadness applied, a slow-release emotion, somehow manageable. I had the time, while watching it disappear, to realize how precious everything was. Had been.

2. Splitting

When my divorce papers arrived, on the day of St. Valentine, with the evening mail, I sat on the floor. On the sill of my kitchen backdoor, to be exact, opening on a narrow hallway facing a wall. On the phone, as I was reporting the news, a friend urged me to celebrate. Should we toast, have a glass of champagne? I was horrified.

After pondering long and deep I had concluded that divorce, the end of any relationship, is the saddest of things except for untimely death. The latter tops it all but splitting from a loved one, even when love is over, is a tight run-upper. No, I shall not celebrate.

Maybe mourn again, as the worst of it had happened years before, when I resolved to separate from my husband. As my intention solidified, once I was in a store with my child, buying a card for Father's Day. The boy's eagerness, enthusiasm and innocence so clashed with my awareness of impending diaspora, I felt petrified on the spot. I knew, and the boy didn't, this small ritual will never be the same. Maybe with some luck it will be repeated. Perhaps we'll still buy presents for Dad. But the context of such gesture will be entirely changed, unavoidably altered. Uglier.

Suddenly, the child's universe as it presently was looked like a crystal egg, unbelievably fragile, also iridescent and beautiful. Perfect, integer, at least to the eyes of the child. And I was about to crush it, to destroy it by leaving. As I looked at the cards displayed on the rack I felt like an automaton, paralyzed by regret, guilt and pain. Plus, again, the most ineffable sadness.

3. Dumping

I used to be the one who could decide to go away. Lift the anchors, hoist the sails, say goodbye. I used to be the one who didn't mind peeling off the bandage, as it must be done and the sting is short-lived.

Once, a boyfriend dumped me. I liked him and enjoyed our relationship. I hadn't seen the end coming. I was surprised and dismayed. Very briefly. In fact, as I had never been ditched before, I discovered how easier it was to be confronted with dismissal than to perform the cut. How the sorrow of abandonment is faster absorbed, because there is no alternative. I healed of being left way more rapidly than I ever recovered from leaving.

Two weeks later, my ex-boyfriend called me in order to hook up again. I was mystified. He said he hadn't meant to split up, truly. He explained it was just, strategy I guess? A move, like if we were playing chess. I was confused and upset. But I couldn't step back.

I had cut the cord as requested, then I had cauterized the wound. It had scarred. You see, I had never conceived one could leave for fun, for a game of hide and seek, perhaps peek-a-boo. I thought it was for good, no other options.

4. Fleeing

I don't miss my homeland. I know it exists. It will not die. I will. My homeland will not remember me. I recall it with love. "It" (my country of origin) doesn't reciprocate. It can't. It is lovely, not loving. Not its fault. It is lovely and always will, independently from my witnessing. Yet I like to witness its loveliness, its unique, tender beauty. Unique, moving, touching, because I know it so well.

I do witness it each time I return to visit my folks. I like watching the land approach as the plane loses elevation. I am impressed by finding it there, the same, equal to itself. Such persistency seems especially generous because of my defection. My land doesn't reject me, in spite of my absence. It still lets me in, blesses me with its cozy, comforting decipherability.

I like watching it as I leave, the plane lifting higher and higher. How it becomes small and undetermined. Yet, again, I am impressed by its gift of permanence. No matter how far I'll fly it will keep in place, resemble itself, be there when I'll return.

But I don't miss my homeland, and I know our stance is reciprocal.

I believe my siblings resent me, because I left home and never came back. Which you can't foresee when somebody goes. "Never came back" can be stated only after the fact. Actually, at the very end of the line, where death dwells.

The absent, says a song, is always wrong. True. It might be why long ago I chose to be that person. To ensure my un-righteousness and un-respectability. In order to be respected, as the word implies, you need to be chest-to-chest with someone. Face to face, ready for "confrontation," an activity I truly detest. I'd rather desert.

Like the dead, the absent is always wrong. Would it help to say that the absent is actually present, necessarily so, somewhere else? Clearly, there are different categories of "where." There are "where(s)" as remote as the underworld. They don't count.

My siblings do not care about my whereabouts. My homeland doesn't either. Does it (my land of origins) feel betrayed? Did I betray it by leaving? It doesn't care. Lands are kind of insensitive if, as I explained, extremely lovely. All of them, lands of departure, of arrival. Your own, other lands that become your own.

Or they don't. I, for instance, don't own any. That is why I am awed by all. Every step, every stand, has become exceptional.

LETTERS

She revealed with delight she had a cousin in the US. Her name was Grace, she said. Emigrated long ago and yet faithfully writing, decade after decade. Such affection from someone who had upgraded, changed status, having moved to a part of the world meaning glamour and wealth, without need for verification, made her unbelievably proud.

Grandma knew nothing about cousin's finances or lifestyle, but the mere fact of being "American" put her relative on a pedestal. Having thrived in a mythical land where all was magnified, people included, warranted her a sort of badge of honor, sparkling gold.

Grace's letters didn't mention any kind of event. For what I recall they were just an orderly list of greetings. She addressed everyone she could think of on our side of the sea, on account of everyone who was there. Those endless regards filled Grandma with joy. You would have told she wasn't cataloguing relatives but reading the Torah, the Psalms, getting deeply in touch with her past and future, with the map of her human belonging.

What I most remember of those flimsy missives is the signature on which Grandma lingered, ecstatic, probably as a means not to part from the whole experience. She was puzzled by the G of cousin's initial, traced in a slightly different style from what the nuns taught in school. That G read as an I, so she wondered about the name Irace with great awe. Strange, she said, did you notice? They don't say Grace overseas! They say Irace.

That sounded exciting, exotic, but alas I had a sense of Grandma being wrong. Lacking serious, old-fashioned calligraphy training, often hesitating on tricky capital letters, I could easily conceive handwriting ambiguities. I suspected cousin Grace to be cousin Grace on either side of the ocean. But I never told Grandma.

Truly, Irace would be a contradiction of terms, juxtaposing anger and sweetness. Who could be called that? Only a mythological creature, an amazon, a mermaid... Anything could happen though, once you passed the Atlantic to never return. Sending back these things thin and precious, these black notes on vellum, fragile threads creating the legend, stretched over oblivion.

Acknowledgments

These proses, or earlier versions of them, appeared in the following publications:

Aji: "Trilogy of Loss"
Alebrijes: "The Tree"
The Blue Tiger Review: "Young Penelope"
Burningword: "Cherries"
The Birds We Piled Loosely: "Her Kind," "Impressions"
Claudius Speaks: "Gardens"
Dragon Poet: "Education," "Lesson"
Eastern Iowa Review: "Vertigo"
Fishfood: "Book of Hours," "Letters"
Five on the Fifth: "Wounded"
FLAR: "Uncaged"
GNU: "Genesis"
Goodworks: "Lorelei"
The Harpoon Review: "Lies they Tell"
Independent Noise: "Page of a Broken Diary"
Indiana Voice: "In the Water"
Indicia: "Ferryboat"
Infinite Rust: "Leaving"
Linden Avenue: "The Ride"
Metafore: "Concentric Circles"
The Minola Review: "Awake"
The Minetta Review: "Dead Brother"
The Nassau Review: "Nicotine"
O:JA&L: "In Tongues"
Pacific Review: "Dynasty"
Panoplyzine: "Wisteria"
poeticdiversity: "Genealogy," "Open Wounds," "The Name"
Random Sample: "Bronte," "Girl by the Window"
The Rathalla Review: "Night Vision"
River Poets: "Ariadne's Song"
The Sierra Nevada Review: "Cameo," "Lament"

Soundings East: "Salt of the Earth"
Subprimal: "Island," "The Same"
Sum: "Nightwatch"
Synesthesia Journal: "The Window"
Thin Air: "Writer"
Thrice Fiction: "The Thing I Am"
Voices of Eve: "Homespun"
Welter Skelter: "Like a Train"
The Write Place at The Write Time: "My Father's Scream,"
"Rumor," "Travelers"

Pski's Porch Publishing was formed July 2012, to make books for people who like people who like books. We hope we have some small successes.

Pski's Porch

323 East Avenue
Lockport, NY 14094
www.pskisporch.com

www.ingramcontent.com/pod-product-compliance
Lightning Source LLC
La Vergne TN
LVHW051737080426
835511LV00018B/3110

* 9 7 8 1 9 4 8 9 2 0 2 8 5 *